Henry Gaylord Wilshire

The Millionaire Socialist

Lou Rosen

School Justice Institute, Publisher
P.O. Box 1270 Pacific Palisades, CA
Rosenlouis53@gmail.com

Library of Congress Catalog Card No. 201191

ISBN 13-# 978-0-615-52124-4

10-#0963382500

*Cover photo courtesy of University of Southern California,
on behalf of the Department of Special Collections
and the California Historical Society*

Acknowledgments

I wish to thank my wife Karen for all her encouragement and patience in living with Henry Gaylord Wilshire at the breakfast and dinner table. I also want to thank Melissa Bauman for the wonderful job she did with the editing and Malena Marie Luongo for her colorful cover design. Help with peer reviews happened with the help of Syd and Cathie Brown, Prescilla Tedesco, Bruce Jugan, Walt and Patty Schwartz, Tom Giuffrida, and my three children, Matt, Brad and Stacey. There were also loads of friends who gave encouragement and support. I am especially thankful to the librarians, photo curators, museum directors and book experts who gave so willingly of their knowledge and resources. I also want to thank my calico cat Lady Gwendolyn who patiently sat beside me during the entire writing process.

Authors Notation

The places, people and events in this book are factual. The dialogue included in several chapters and the epilogue is fictitious but certainly could have occurred. Chapter Seven is the result of a trip the author made to Bishop and the Cardinal Creek Gold Mine in May 2010 and several people he spoke to about Wilshire and the mine. The author apologizes for any offense to descendants of people described or for insensitive geographic names used at the time. The goal is to not offend but to make the content as historically accurate as possible.

Contents

Introduction

The name Wilshire is known primarily as a street in Los Angeles that is famous all over the world. A name often associated with prestige and quality, "Wilshire" adorns the signs of hundreds of hotels, jewelry stores, apartment houses, clothing stores and insurance companies. Who was Henry Gaylord Wilshire? How did his name get on one of the most famous streets in the world? Why was he called "the Millionaire Socialist?" Does he deserve to be famous?

Henry Gaylord Wilshire's life reads like a novel. How many individuals have run for Congress in two different states, for Parliament in both Great Britain and Canada, and for attorney general of New York State? How many have had the courage to publish a socialist magazine that irritated both the government and the media and at one time had the largest circulation of any socialist journal in the world? How many men have counted as friends such literary luminaries as Jack London, George Bernard Shaw, and Upton Sinclair? Wilshire was all of those things. Was he also a con man who invented a magnetic belt that he claimed could cure cancer, diabetes, baldness and constipation? Was he a swindler who sold $2.6 million of stock in a gold mine alleging it would eliminate the national debt?

Dreamers are a dime a dozen. We are all dreamers to some extent. But it is one thing to dream about going to the moon and another to buy a ticket. Wilshire bought a lifetime pass. Though many of his dreams did not come true, the joy of pursuing them was written all over him.

This book is not just a biography of a well-known figure in Los Angeles history. The man certainly deserves our attention, but the book is also about the era in which Wilshire lived. The later part of the nineteenth century and the beginning of the twentieth century in the United States was a time of skepticism about capitalism and social Darwinism. It was a time of new inventions and wild real estate investments. It was a time of robber barons—named for business practices built on monopolies and unscrupulous trusts—as well as labor unions and socialism. America after the Civil War was using the products of the Industrial Revolution to build large cities, railroads, and steel mills. Gone were the pioneers, mountain men, and gold miners. Taking their place were entrepreneurs, investors, and engineers.

Henry Gaylord Wilshire was not trained as an engineer, a publisher, or a politician. But he never let lack of training interfere with his ambition and tremendous ego. The Yiddish word "chutzpah" best describes the Millionaire Socialist. He had nerve, ambition, and a tremendous desire to achieve something great. He was also impatient and not always trustworthy. Wilshire had empathy for the workingman but concern for preserving capitalism despite being a socialist. He had many friends, and although he was not famous, he was certainly well-known among socialists and business leaders in Los Angeles, New York, and San Francisco. To many he was a pest and self-promoter. He was even called the P.T Barnum of socialism for his ability to sell the philosophy. To others he was a genius. He was certainly intelligent, well-read, and well-traveled. He was not a drunkard, a womanizer, or a thief, but he was perhaps unethical at times and took advantage of trusting friends.

Wilshire was indisputably successful at one thing: prophesizing the future. He didn't expand Wilshire Boulevard to the ocean, but he converted an abandoned 35-acre barley field into the beginnings of a thoroughfare that would connect downtown Los Angeles to the sea. He did not invent the automobile, but he predicted the city would someday be developed around roads and thoroughfares. He did not create Social Security, Medicare, and unemployment insurance, but he predicted they would exist.

Was Wilshire a villain or a man ahead of his time? Did he sell thousands of shares in an electric belt knowing it was a fake, or did he invent a device that really cured people? Did he sell millions of dollars' worth of shares in a gold mine that was a big con, or would the mine have paid off if he had had more resources? Was his brand of socialism just for show, or was it a precursor to the Democratic Party and progressive platforms of modern times? Does the name Millionaire Socialist really describe him, or does the fact that he made six fortunes during his life and lost them all make the title dubious? Was he a dangerous change agent or just a showoff? Was he a Don Quixote or Neitzsche's man of the future? Readers must answer those questions for themselves.

CHAPTER 1
A Rich Man's Son Comes of Age

It was a beautiful walk down the familiar Cincinnati street on that crisp fall Sunday afternoon. The air smelled of wet leaves and pot roast as families gathered for their after-church meal. Though his stomach was growling, Henry Gaylord Wilshire was glad he had chosen to walk the four miles home from the train station. But it wasn't because he was enjoying the weather; Henry needed time to prepare himself.

There are lots of things in this world to fear. Perhaps one of the scariest is telling your parent something they won't want to hear, even one as loving and caring as Henry Gaylord Wilshire's father. At twenty, the son had come to the decision that Harvard University was not for him. His father, George, was tremendously proud that Henry was attending Harvard. Lacking a college education himself, George Wilshire always felt a little inferior to those who had one, and he believed higher education was important for all three of his sons. Henry hated to disappoint his father, but his mind was made up. His palms began to sweat, and moisture formed on his brow as he pondered confronting his father.

Henry was not a coward, but this was different. He loved and wanted to please his father, but he simply could not bring himself to return to the terrible boredom that was Harvard. Too bad he didn't have an excuse to leave—an illness or a war to go fight. He wished his mother were alive. Women protected their young, and God knows he needed protecting.

Henry became more introspective the farther he walked. Sometimes it is difficult to know what you really want. He knew for sure he was miserable trying to be what his father wanted him to be. It was true that a professor would occasionally make him think. One instructor, William James, who wrote *The Sentiment of Reality*, once told the class, "We do not know what draughts may blow in upon our back, what doors may open, what forms may enter, what interesting objects may be found in cupboards and corners." Henry liked that sentence. There were certainly many interesting corners of his mind to explore, and he certainly wanted draughts blowing upon his back. After all, it was 1882—a time of opportunity. One could become rich and famous with nerve, intelligence, and contacts. He knew he had those in spades.

Henry liked the social part of Harvard. He liked the smart, sophisticated young men he had met, and the rich and famous graduates he had encountered at parties and bars. Henry had learned to play a new game called golf, to dance with beautiful women, and to speak with a moneyed accent. He absorbed enough in class to talk like an educated man, even if it was mostly hot air. If you sounded like you knew what you were talking about, he discovered, people usually listened. Henry also learned to ride, becoming a pretty good horseman. He dressed well, knew about fine wines and whiskeys, and could choose a good cigar. He liked his women beautiful and well-informed. There were plenty of those in Boston.

A passable student, Henry had excelled in economics. He had even been asked to present his paper on the growing divide between rich and poor in America to his economics class, receiving congratulations and plaudits from his fellow students. On the other hand, biology, Latin, ancient history, English literature, and trigonometry held no fascination for him. He lacked the patience to truly become an educated man. He once read that Ralph Waldo Emerson had said, "Books are for the scholar's idle times." He thought ol' Waldo had something there.

Henry knew he could not compete with his father's success. George Wilshire, a millionaire, served on the board of directors of six major businesses, owned a bank and three small railroads, and helped found Standard Oil of Ohio. Worshipped in the world of business, George came from humble beginnings and had only an elementary school education. His ancestors came to the United States from Somersetshire, England, in 1805. George was born in Maine and worked on a farm until he was nineteen. He was a restless young man and set out for "the far west" Ohio territory in 1837. When he got to Ohio, he went into business with his brother. Both brothers were known as active, energetic, and careful, but George soon gained a reputation as being unusually resourceful and keen at recognizing promising new ventures. He became director of the Fireman's Insurance Company, Saint Louis and Chicago Rail, Sandusky and Cleveland Rail, and Cincinnati Light and Cable, as well as president of the Third National Bank of Cincinnati. He also owned Newport Iron and Pipe Company in nearby Cleveland. In 1850 George married Sarah Clemens of Covington, Kentucky, a cousin of Samuel Clemens (Mark Twain). She died in 1862, not long after Henry, their youngest son, was born. George Wilshire was one of the most respected businessmen in Ohio. He was known to be honest, resourceful, and keenly aware of where the country was headed.

It was no wonder Henry was nervous.

He wondered what words he would use to persuade his father to let him withdraw from Harvard. Henry's father had counted on his sons taking over his business interests. The eldest, George Jr., sat on the board of directors of his father's bank and was doing an excellent job of being the son of an icon. Henry's sister, Clara, had married well, and her husband was active in two of her father's railroads. William, the middle son, convinced his father there was money to be made in California. He had contacted some of his father's friends and was purchasing a small safe and scale company in San Francisco.

In some ways Henry was like his father: adventurous and unafraid to try something new. But he lacked his father's patience and discipline. Why learn about a venture from the ground up when you could learn it from the top down? People made too much of the need for experience. All you needed be successful was a little luck and a little nerve, Henry thought. He decided to use that argument with his father.

The Wilshire house on Fourth Street was typical of many Richardsonian Romanesque mansions on the block.

It was a stately house but not ostentatious. The home had two large turrets, seven chimneys, a large front porch that wrapped around two sides of the house. Large windows dominated all sides, and gargoyles stared down from the eaves. Light blue with white trim around the windows, the mansion boasted seven bedrooms, six baths, a huge kitchen, a parlor, a pool table room, and a large library and study. There were large trees in front of the house and on the long sweeping lawn in back. The house across the street belonged to the Tafts, whose young son William Howard, a lawyer, was being groomed by the Republican Party as a candidate for Congress.

Source: Library of Congress
STATELY STYLE: Richardsonian Romanesque was a popular architectural style in the Wilshire' Cincinnati neighborhood. This example is the house of James J. Hill.

Henry had spent most of his childhood in the family home in Cincinnati. He remembered climbing the big sycamore in the back yard and watching his older brother hang two ropes to build a wide plank swing for William and him. Henry fell off once when he went too high and nearly broke an arm. He remembered playing croquet with his father and his friends, and drinking lemonade in the summertime on the patio. He recalled hiding from his father once when he didn't want to come in for supper. He now had a similar feeling. Was it too late to go hide?

He entered the front door and heard his father's voice coming from the front parlor.

"Good afternoon, Henry. I saw you coming down the walk. I wish I could say I am glad to see you, but I am not. I received your letter. You have made a terrible decision."

"Father, you know I would not do anything to hurt or dishonor you. I have always tried to be a good son. I know you wanted me to follow in George's footsteps, but banking is not for me. Neither is Harvard. I sat in class after class of boring, useless lectures. I listened to vain and impractical men talk about subjects that had no interest for me. I hated Harvard from the very first day. I only endured a year of it to please you. I just cannot force myself to go on."

There was a long silence before his father responded. "I want for you something I was not able to have—a university education. I would have given anything to have the chance to be exposed to the kind of education you are rejecting."

Henry replied, "I understand why this is important to you. I thought about it a great deal at Harvard. But I want something else. To be honest I don't know what that is, but I do know that I do not want to waste any more time in a classroom."

As George listened, the wrinkles in his forehead deepened. "Henry, you know I love you as much as a man can love a son. My children mean everything to me. My businesses also mean something to me. They represent more than money; they represent what I have achieved in my life. Even if I lose everything I will know that I created thousands of jobs and a great deal of wealth. I created something honest and worthwhile. That is what I want to pass on to you. Is that such a bad thing?"

"It is certainly not a bad thing, but your interests are not my interests. Your businesses are not my businesses." Another long pause settled in between the young man and his father.

George broke the silence. "Henry, I have never told anyone this before. I do know what you are feeling. My father wanted me to take over the family farm when I was your age. I am not a lazy man, but farming is mostly physical, and I have a good mind. I knew at an early age that I was smarter than most people. Even in the small town in Maine where I was raised I saw many opportunities to do things better and more efficiently. I came to my father as you are coming to me now. I told him farming was not for me, and I wanted to move out west to Ohio. He never forgave me. He never spoke to me again. I do not want that to happen to you and me."

Henry nearly collapsed with relief. "Father, hearing that story helps me more than you can know. I dreaded coming here today. I feel closer to you right now than I have ever felt before. We are talking now not as father and son but as two men."

The older man smiled and said, "Two handsome and brilliant men I might add."

They laughed, and Henry said, "Father, you will not be sorry. Harvard is a good place for philosophers and academics, but I am neither. What would you think if I went to California with William and partnered with him in the safe and scale business?"

"I need to think about that," his father said. "Remember, William finished Harvard, and my helping finance his business venture was his graduation present. What have you done to deserve a gift?"

"Not much, I know," Henry replied. "This would not be so much a gift but an investment. I hope you want to make an investment in my potential. Surely you know I have talents that have not been tapped."

George chuckled. "Henry, you have more charm and personality than any of my children. I believe you could charm the rattles off a snake, but it is the untapped potential you mentioned that concerns me. You are not a heavy drinker, a gambler, or a womanizer, but you have a certain wild streak I do not understand. You have always been attracted to rather odd people. Not bad people but people who march to a different drummer than most of us. Perhaps if you were introduced to practical people who work hard for a living, it might influence the way you think."

There was another slight pause in the conversation, and the older man said, "Henry, I have a proposition for you. You say you want to try something entirely different. What would you say to working in my small rolling stock mill in Cleveland? You could see how steel is made and learn something about the business from the ground up. I am not suggesting you start on the steel mill floor with the hired hands. You would work under Bob Underwood, the plant manager. You would learn not only how steel is made but also how it is sold and what new technologies are just around the corner. If you give it an honest try and it does not work out, I will let you join William in San Francisco."

Hesitantly, Henry said, "I am willing to give making steel a try. I remember Bob Underwood. He is a nice man and seems smart and innovative." Henry was not really enthusiastic, but he knew he shouldn't push his luck. It might be interesting for a time, and perhaps living alone in a new environment and making new friends would be good for him.

"Bob Underwood is using a new electroplating technique that could revolutionize how steel is made," George said. "You could learn a lot from him. That mill is making more profit than all three of my railroads. I am disappointed in your not wanting to pursue Harvard, but it would cushion the blow if you learned the steel business and made the mill prosper. We have a small house in Anatolia, a little town near Cleveland, not too far from the mill. You could stay there. I think you would like the area."

Henry decided that feigned enthusiasm was the better part of valor and said, "I need something besides musty old professors and claustrophobic classrooms. I think Cleveland and steelmaking may be just the thing. Thank you for being so understanding. I am lucky to have a father like you."

"Thank me after you see what you are getting into. Things are changing in the business world. It's a Darwinian competition in which only the fittest survive. Success in business today means you have to swallow your pride and sometimes your ethics. You need to be brutal to some extent. I think you will learn that in Cleveland, and it may be more useful than anything you could learn at Harvard. I only hope you are tough enough."

***

As Henry left his father's house that afternoon, he wondered what his father meant about toughness. He always thought of businessmen as well-dressed, polished, and polite gentlemen who played golf, belonged to the best clubs, and had a haircut every ten days. Being tough sounded like a working man's trait. He had never given a thought to being tough; he wasn't sure he really knew the meaning of the word.

Henry left for Cleveland the next week. When he got off the train, he asked the cabbie to drive through the downtown area to the steel mills before taking him to Anatolia. Cleveland was on the edge of Lake Erie, a brown, muddy body of water that was anything but beautiful but was impressive in size. Cleveland was not as large as Cincinnati but had more industry. Steel mills lined the Cuyahoga River, and the smokestacks belched vast columns of gray mist. The downtown area was growing quickly, with buildings going up everywhere. The streets were wide and many were paved. It was a thriving young city that oozed promise.

When Henry arrived in Anatolia, it brought back memories of childhood. The family had taken several summer vacations there, and he remembered boat races, swimming, and ice cream down by the lake. Anatolia, named after an ancient archeological site in Turkey, was known locally for an excellent Turkish restaurant. Henry later learned that Turkey's Anatolia might have been where steel originated. More of a neighborhood than a town, Anatolia was in the Cleveland Heights area and was more commonly known as Shaker Heights. There were several large, stylish homes in the area, but the Wilshire home was less grand, as it was primarily a vacation house rather than a permanent residence.

Henry had cabled Bob Underwood to say he was coming to work at the mill. Bob had cabled back, saying George had told him all about it and he was looking forward to seeing Henry. Henry decided he wanted to see the mill first thing in the morning.

The next day Henry arrived at the mill. It was not nearly as large as other mills you could see down by the river. Cities like Akron, Canton, and Youngstown were springing up just south of Cleveland, each based on steel and iron making. Ohio was a pioneer in the emerging steel industry. The first Bessemer converter, a new device for steel manufacturers, was produced by the Cleveland Rolling Mill Company, a rival of George Wilshire's Newport Pipe and Cable Company. But Newport Pipe and Cable was a smaller specialty mill that produced quality pipe for the building industry and cable for the shipping industry. George Wilshire had no intention of competing with the large new steel mills. He had found a niche in the market, and he knew it. In 1875 the first open-hearth furnace was built exclusively for the Otis Steel Company in Cleveland. Open-hearth furnaces were expensive to build—too expensive for George Wilshire, who was more interested in his bank and railroads than he was in making steel.

Henry was impressed with the green lawn and trees in front of Newport Pipe and Cable. The light blue building was newly painted, the walks were clean, and the windows sparkled. Out back he could see the mill and the chimneys pumping out big clouds of smoke. He could hear the sound of metal on metal, and could see horses and mules pulling heavy loads of pipe and cable from the passageways alongside of the large tin buildings.

He entered the office and was greeted by a pretty, petite secretary who blushed when he told her his name. The name Wilshire was magic in these parts. She disappeared into another office and out came Bob Underwood. Underwood was a large man with big hands and a heart to match. He wore a long mustache, waxed at the ends, and parted his hair in the middle. He wore no coat but had on a striped shirt and a brace of wide suspenders.

"Henry, it is good to see you. It has been a while, hasn't it? You are looking fit."

"Hello, Bob, it is good to see you, too. I take it my father told you why I am here."

"Yes, he did. I think it will be a good experience for you. College is fine, but there is nothing better than real life experience."

"I agree. So where do I begin?"

"I thought I would start you off with a shovel and a hot furnace. Have you got any work gloves?"

"I hope you are kidding," Henry said. "I am not used to using my back instead of my brain. However, I do want to see how steel is made. I have read a little about it but not enough."

"I am only half kidding. It might do you good to get your hands dirty. Making steel is hard labor, and working on the floor would teach you a lot. In any case, you should start by reading about the process and the history of the industry. I have an office set up for you full of books. I think you should spend at least three days reading and studying. Once you have the foundation, you can go into the mill and observe the process first-hand. I have assigned a foreman to show you around."

Underwood led Henry down the hall to a smaller office and a desk stacked with books. The room smelled like ash and dust, but it was kind of cozy, the chair was comfortable, and the light was good. Henry liked learning about practical things and was actually excited to learn how steel was made. The noise from the mill was horrendous, but Henry decided it added to the atmosphere.

Henry settled into reading and taking notes. Underwood's wife was a schoolteacher, and she may have had a hand in choosing the reading materials. There were books on the history of steelmaking and metallurgy. There were volumes on chemistry and thermodynamics. Some were over Henry's head, but he absorbed enough to get a general idea of the history of steel and how it was made.

Henry learned that iron was mined in several states. Mining iron begins at ground level and originates in taconite rock. Taconite rock is 28 percent iron; the rest is sand or silica. Once mined, the taconite is ground into a fine powder and mixed with water. A series of magnets grabs the iron particles, and the rest is discarded. For every ton of iron retained, two tons of water, or tailings, are discarded. The crude taconite is delivered to large gyrator crushers, where chunks as large as five feet are reduced to six inches or less. More than 6,000 tons of taconite can be crushed in one hour. The crushed material is transferred by conveyor belt to an ore storage building. A feeder sends the ore to the concentrator building for grinding, separating, and concentrating. Eventually the iron is turned into steel pellets.

Henry also learned that steel is an alloy consisting mostly of iron and carbon. It is usually 5 percent nickel, manganese, chromium, vanadium and tungsten, and 95 percent iron. Carbon and some of the other metals act as hardening agents. Steelmakers vary the amount of carbon if they want increased harness or strength. The iron looks like red sand, while the other metals resemble yellow sand.

In one of the history books, Henry learned that steel has been produced for centuries, long before the Renaissance. Its use became common after more efficient production methods were devised in the seventeenth century. The earliest known site of steel production was in Anatolia, Turkey, circa 2000 B.C. Evidence of steelmaking has also been found in East Africa dating to 1400 B.C., and steel weapons were produced in the Iberian Peninsula in the fourth century. Roman soldiers wielded steel swords.

Technology continued to improve, and steelmaking became easier and cheaper during the Industrial Revolution. Once manufacturers learned how to extract the oxygen from the ore, a process known as smelting, they could make a metal known as pig iron. Once they could manufacture pig iron, they could add other metals to the mixture to make various kinds of steel. Since the seventeenth century the smelting of iron ore into pig iron was done in an extremely hot "blast furnace" stoked by either coke or charcoal. With the invention of the Bessemer process in the mid-nineteenth century, steel became an inexpensive mass-produced material, nearly as cheap as cast iron.

The Bessemer process was the first inexpensive industrial process for the mass production of steel from molten pig iron. The process is named after its inventor, Henry Bessemer, who took out a patent on the process in 1855. The process removes the impurities from iron by oxidation with the air, which raises the temperature of the iron mass and keeps it molten with much less fuel. The cost of making steel was greatly influenced by fuel used to melt the iron and keep it molten. Henry knew that Newport Pipe and Cable primarily used coke as the heating agent because it was cheaper than coal. He had seen mounds of used coke from the blast furnaces being loaded onto open railroad cars.

One book explained how various temperatures and cooling processes bolstered the strength of the steel. The liquid steel is poured into long casts that produce steel slabs or ingots. The steel slabs can be hot rolled or cold rolled into long flat sheets. Other cuts of steel are made into specialized forms such as I-beams or rails. At Newport Pipe and Cable, the steel was sheet rolled, and the thin sheets were folded into various diameters of pipe and seam welded. In the early days, welders performed the task. Other specialized steel was rolled into wire of various sizes, and then wound into cable.

Henry read about the new electric arc furnaces that were able to melt scrap metal and use the molten metal to create new steel. This method would bypass extracting the iron ore from taconite and would soon be worth a fortune to the mills that used it. The problem was the electric arc furnace required a great deal of electricity, and electricity in 1882 Cleveland was expensive.

Henry was thrilled with what he was learning. One text indicated that some of the techniques for extracting iron from taconite were being used to remove gold from rock formations. It was a fact he squirreled away in his memory. There would come a day when this knowledge would be extremely helpful.

After three days of intense study, Henry felt ready. He was amazed at how quickly he had come to understand the process. Henry went to Underwood and told him he had mastered steelmaking. It was time to go to the mill and tell the men what they were doing wrong. Underwood laughed, and gave him a helmet and some goggles. He then called in a foreman named Jessie, who shook Henry's hand. His hands felt like sandpaper, and his body looked as hard as the steel he was making. Jessie was not a talker. He motioned for Henry to follow him.

They went into the mill, and the heat and noise struck Henry immediately. The heat was coming from giant cup-shaped metal containers called crucibles. Nearly white-hot molten liquid was being poured from the crucibles into molds. Noise loud enough to damage your eardrums was coming from a nearby room. Henry wished he had put cotton in his ears. It was useless trying to talk or ask Jessie questions, but he could figure out most of what he was seeing.

Source: Library of Congress Photo Collection
ORE-INSPIRED ART: A drawing by Charles Graham in 1886 depicts the steaming cauldrons and molded ingots of the steel-making process at the time.

Henry saw conveyor belts carrying what must have been iron ore to a high platform and three men shoveling it into another large crucible. The power from belching steam engines on the floor was channeled into lifting and turning the crucible.

On a second platform were several large open containers, which he assumed contained raw materials for making other metals. He climbed a ladder to peer into the steel cauldron. The liquid was a beautiful molten red. Very little smoke was coming off the liquid, but heat was a different matter. It singed Henry's eyebrows and eyelashes, and Jessie motioned not to get so close to the edge of the crucible. He noticed a small amount of sludge floating on top of the molten steel. Three large men were putting yellow sand metal ores into the cauldron. They had been doing it for years and like a good cook did not need a recipe.

A clanging sound was coming from a room just beyond where Henry was standing. Curious, he walked inside and saw that steam power was lifting a huge metal sledgehammer and letting it fall onto large ingots below. He had read that the more you hammered an ingot the stronger it became.

Henry tired after watching the process for several hours. He motioned to Jessie and went back to his office to absorb what he had seen. He now understood that making steel was complicated. Making good steel was even more complicated. Really understanding the process took a good knowledge of chemistry. He would need to study more and observe the floor many times to truly understand.

On the weekends Henry tried to get out and meet people. He was a social creature and was happiest in a crowd. Anatolia was a wealthy and religious community. Both adjectives applied to Henry's next-door neighbors, a friendly banker and his wife. They invited Henry to join them at their church one Sunday. The church was Pentecostal, which meant adherents interpreted the Bible literally and sometimes spoke in tongues. Henry thought religion was ridiculous for the most part although he liked the hymns of the Wesleyans and the Gregorian chants of the Catholics. The idea that people accepted myth as truth was incomprehensible to him. A man walking on water, a woman turning into a pillar of salt, and water parting so the good guys could get away seemed like childish fairy tales to Henry. But he realized that most Americans were religious and that he needed to accept it as a fact of life.

At church, his neighbors John and Molly introduced him to one the most beautiful girls he had ever seen. Her name was Joan. She had light brown hair, green eyes and a fantastic body. She wore the empire-waisted dress of the day, which made a woman's waist look tiny and her breasts large, though in Joan's cases, the flattering style was unnecessary. Henry began to have urges ten minutes after he met her. He knew he had to get to know her better.

Henry tried his best imitation of a clean-living Christian conversationalist.

"I am pleased to meet you, Joan. My neighbors tell me you are a full-time resident of Anatolia. I lived here during the summer as a kid. I liked it then and I like it now."

The beautiful girl smiled and said, "It is a lovely little town. I hope you stay a while. I think you will like it here."

Henry thought to himself, "I will like it here if I can look at you every day. Your eyes are the color of the green aggies I used to have when I played marbles down by the lake. Your mouth was made to kiss. My God, what a beautiful face."

Out loud, he said, "Tell me, Joan, what do you do with your time? Do you ever go to the famous Anatolia Restaurant?"

"My father takes me there for my birthday, and occasionally we take visitors there. Have you been lately?"

"I have not eaten there in a long time. Is it as good as ever?"

"It is wonderful. Perhaps you and I could accompany father and your neighbors there sometime?"

"I would like that," Henry replied.

Henry and Joan would eat at the Anatolia several times, with her father and sometimes alone. They gradually became an item despite his rejecting Joan's constant urging for him to attend church.

Her lips proved to be kissable, but he was too much of a gentleman to press hard for more. He settled for the occasional kiss and hand-holding while they walked.

They were an attractive couple from good families, and it seemed to be a match made in heaven. But there were problems in paradise. Joan was very religious and did not drink. Henry was no lush, but he liked a glass of wine with dinner and an occasional shot of whiskey with the boys. Joan badgered Henry about taking Jesus Christ as his savior and urged him to attend church with her not only on Sunday but also twice during the week. Henry soon decided that Christ was not really his savior and that Joan and her father were just too religious for him. He broke it off and suspected Joan was as relieved as he was. He often toasted her great figure and beautiful face with a glass of good wine.

After four months in Anatolia, Henry began to look for ways to improve productivity at Newport Pipe and Cable. He knew the new electric arc furnaces were one solution, but the mill would need to generate its own electricity. If he could build an electrical generating plant using the water from Lake Erie, Henry knew he could sell electricity to the local mills. He began to study what it would take to build a power plant.

While Henry was thinking of new ways to make steel, Andrew Carnegie, the great steel magnate and one of the richest men in the world, decided it was time to get rid of some of his smaller competitors. He lowered the price of steel to a level that broke most smaller mills. Newport Pipe and Cable had a corner on the pipe and cable market but still lost much of its business to Carnegie's trust-like tactics.

The 1880s and '90s in the United States were the height of the trusts. The Industrial Revolution was in full swing after the Civil War. Hundreds of new technologies and products were being developed, and thousands of small industries were emerging in states like Ohio, Illinois, and Pennsylvania. New entrepreneurs were eager to make their fortunes. The combination of new products and new fortune seekers resulted in a glut of both. In the opinion of the super-rich, small industries needed to be weeded out from time to time.

Combinations of industries were forbidden by law, but certain industries were allowed to form "pools" of the principal manufacturers with an eye toward limiting production and thus maintaining high prices. Some of those industries were owned by men who would become giants of American capitalism: McCormick in agricultural machinery; Carnegie in steel; Rockefeller in oil; Armor, Swift, Wilson, and Hammond in meatpacking; Westinghouse in electrical equipment; Havemeyer and Spreckels in sugar; Duke and Reynolds in tobacco; the Guggenheims in copper; Weyerhaeuser in lumber; the Mellons in aluminum; Pierpont Morgan in banking and finance; and Ford in automobiles. Then there were the railroad barons Vanderbilt, Scott, and the Pacific Associates, and those rising welders of railroad empires, Gould, Hill and Harriman.

These men succeeded because the times were ripe. Most Americans regarded them as builders. The Civil War had transferred large quantities of capital into their shrewd hands. A complacent government let them acquire cheap raw materials, protected them through tariffs and low income taxes, and looked the other way when they applied "survival of the fittest" tactics to smaller competitors.

In the case of the steel industry, Carnegie's main mills were in Pittsburg. Born in Scotland, he was brought to Pittsburgh in 1848 by his family and became a bobbin boy in a cotton mill. Small, shrewd, alert, and cheery, the lad quickly absorbed the national spirit of "go ahead." He became a messenger boy, a telegraph operator, and eventually an official of the Pennsylvania Railroad. He acquired some capital and ventured into the organization and expansion of a forging shop. The venture grew and so did his fortune. The manufacture of cheap, malleable mild steel by the Kelly-Bessemer process had sprung up in a number of places after 1864. Carnegie built a state-of-the-art mill based on the process and began to manufacture steel rails. Carnegie hired Captain William R. Jones, one of the great mechanical and production geniuses of the steel business. His rail business grew exponentially, and he established other mills.

Carnegie formed an alliance with Rockefeller interests and developed ore mines around Lake Superior. Carnegie had a fleet of ore boats so efficient that product mined in Minnesota on Monday morning could be turned into steel rails in Pittsburgh by Saturday night. He was vicious when he needed to be. Carnegie broke agreements with competitors and formed pools that limited where steel was sold. He then lowered the price to force the small mills out of business and raised it again after they went bankrupt—a common tactic of many trusts.

STEEL MAGNATE: Andrew Carnegie forced smaller competitors out of business by lowering his prices only to raise them again after the rivals went bankrupt.

Henry encountered Carnegie's tactics just six months after arriving in Anatolia. Carnegie slashed the price of steel sheeting from his Pittsburgh mills by a third. He could farm out pipe and cable to some of his smaller mills and sell it far cheaper than

Newport Pipe and Cable ever could. It became obvious to Henry that the business was in serious trouble. He took the train to Cincinnati and went to see his father.

George Wilshire was way ahead of him. He knew the trusts' methods inside and out; he was sometimes a partner in their schemes. When a friend inside Carnegie's business told George what Carnegie was up to, he immediately put Newport Pipe and Cable up for sale. He told Henry that he had a European buyer and the mill was in escrow. George did not make money on the sale, but he did not lose any either. It was a good business transaction by a savvy businessman. Henry, however, was furious about Carnegie's tactics—a fury that stayed with him his entire life.

Henry could not believe his father had given in so easily. They should have fought Carnegie tooth and nail, he thought, and perhaps developed and applied new manufacturing techniques that would produce steel in such volume that Carnegie would be the one over a barrel. But Henry was too inexperienced to see the big picture. The mill was a small venture for his father, who had better things to do with his time and money than fight Andrew Carnegie. Besides, George knew and admired Carnegie. Twenty years later Carnegie would sell his steel companies to J. Pierpont Morgan and Company for $4,500,000, making him one of the nation's richest men.

Henry began to read ravenously about the trusts. He learned of their shady and unscrupulous tactics and how they used the capitalist system in a way that would destroy it in the long run. Henry had always believed that people worked best when they worked for their own interests. Self-interest was truer to man's nature than socialism. He had read some of Karl Marx's essays and had once gone to hear Marx's daughter speak. Socialism was appealing, but it was too idealistic and impractical for his tastes. On the other hand, perhaps it held the answer to limiting the power of the trusts.

Then a friend gave him *Progress and Poverty* by Henry George. There were two books that influenced Henry Gaylord Wilshire, and this was one of them. Henry George was born into a poor family of Philadelphia and had traveled widely as a sailor and gold seeker before settling in California as a printer and editor. His travels and experiences caused him to wonder about the great chasm between rich and poor. His book proposed that poverty was caused by wealthy city dwellers purchasing vast amounts of land that they neither lived on nor farmed. They used their wealth to control and exploit the value of land, and earned their wealth not through work or effort but through investment and manipulation.

The remedy was to limit land ownership to those who lived on it and used it. Taxation of anything but land was an unjust penalty levied on production. George proposed a single tax on 100 percent of all income from rents, which would confiscate all "unearned increments" and bring about national ownership of tenements and great estates without rejecting capitalism outright. Here was a philosophy that Henry could believe. It could save capitalism and at the same time end the unfair practices of the wealthy.

Source: Warren J. Samuels Portrait Collection, Duke University
LAND USE: Henry George wrote in Progress and Poverty that poverty
was caused by wealthy city dwellers purchasing vast amounts of land
that they neither lived on nor farmed.

When Henry returned to Anatolia, he learned that he was not the only one who had read *Progress and Poverty.* He was introduced to a small group of enthusiastic believers in a single-tax system who met in an abandoned office building near his home. He also met a doctor named Richard Stoddard and his lovely daughter Grace. Meetings were held every Sunday evening, and the group was mostly young, bright and well-read. Henry began seeing Grace socially. She had a lovely figure and was neither religious nor moralistic. She was great fun to be around. Dr. Stoddard often gave short speeches at the meetings comparing the evils of the state with the evils of disease.

One evening someone asked, "Should the nation own and operate the industries, or should rich capitalists own them?" The discussion came around to the trusts and their greed and unfair practices. The question gradually became: "Should the nation own the trusts?" At subsequent meetings, the group continually came back to the question until it became a kind of mantra. They decided to formally organize, electing Henry president and Grace secretary. They called their group the Nationalist Club. The founding premise was that everyone should have equal opportunity to compete and that the extreme inequality between rich and poor had destroyed that opportunity for those without capital. Members believed that higher taxes on the wealthy and opportunities for education, land ownership, and medical benefits for all were necessary if capitalism was to survive. They decided to run Grace's brother, a young attorney, for the Legislature. He received just twenty-seven votes, but the idea that their group could put one of their own on a ballot was encouraging.

Considering the Nationalist Club's ideas to be socialist, parents and churches discouraged people from having anything to do with the club. Socialists, after all, believed in free love, atheism, and confiscation of wealth. These were values deeply abhorrent to the people of Anatolia. It became obvious that the Nationalist Club's days were numbered, and its members drifted off into other pursuits.

Henry had received a letter from his brother William, who mentioned that Henry should give some thought to joining him in his business venture. He believed they would make a great team: William would be the pragmatic administrator, and Henry would be the creative entrepreneur.

It did not take Henry long to decide that joining William's business in San Francisco was a great idea. He remembered his father's promise to let him join William if the steelmaking business did not work out. He needed to get out of Ohio and the East altogether. California offered fresh, exciting opportunities. He could not wait to get back to Cincinnati and meet with William.

Henry cabled his brother that he was very much interested in his San Francisco offer and that he would return to Cincinnati the next week. Could they meet for lunch at the Atlantic Garden Cafe in the old west end?

Henry packed his bags, said goodbye to Grace and her father, and took the train to Cincinnati. He had only been in Anatolia for three months, but he felt he had obtained a better education in that short time in Anatolia than he ever would have received at Harvard.

***

When he arrived at the family home on C Street, there was a cable from William saying he looked forward to having lunch with Henry the next Wednesday.

The day of the appointment, Henry left the house wondering if the next three months would be as exciting as the last three. He took a horse-drawn trolley to Old Town. The streets were bustling with buggies, trolleys, and even a few of the new horseless carriages. Henry could not believe how much Cincinnati had changed in the past few years. It was now a major city.

Henry loved the friendly people of Cincinnati. They were always good for a smile and a handshake. He saw people of all races and ethnic groups in the streets, including many well-dressed men and women. At one time, Cincinnati was called "Porkerville" by newspaper wags. It was a pork industry hub where hogs were slaughtered and the meat shipped down the Ohio River or across the country by railroad. While the odor of the slaughterhouses was now overpowered by the smell of flowers in the parks and the scent of beautiful women walking down the broad avenues, there was still an element of "The West" just below the polite veneer.

Henry found the Atlantic Garden Café on Third Street, and it was just as he had remembered it. It was both unique enough to attract a young wealthy crowd and delicious enough to attract working men and women. It was originally a German restaurant, thus the emphasis on beer. It still had sawdust on the floor and signs that advertised coffee at two cents a cup. The smell was equal parts baked pork, fresh bread, strong coffee and stale beer. Waiters were carrying large trays filled with pitchers of brew and plates of sandwiches and potato salad. A player piano was plinking out an unfamiliar tune.

Source: Dons Cards, Cincinnati, Ohio
BEER AND BRATS: The Atlantic Garden Cafe, portrayed in this
1885 drawing, was a popular Cincinnati meeting place.

Henry saw William sitting by the window near the door. Across the room were two pretty young women laughing and looking his way. Too bad he and his brother had other things to do, Henry thought. Looking back at William, he noticed his brother had gained a little weight. William was blonder than Henry with a sturdier build. He had a wonderful smile and laugh. You had to like him.

"Hello, brother of mine," Henry said. "Good to see you."

"Henry! It is amazing how fast everything is happening. I am thrilled that you plan to join me," William replied.

"All I needed to hear was 'California.' That word has an attraction all its own. When you throw in 'San Francisco,' how could I refuse?"

"Here is the waiter," William said. "Let's order before you notice those two gorgeous creatures over there and forget why you came here."

Henry laughed and said, "Are you kidding? I noticed them from across the street." Turning to the waiter, he ordered the house special, a porker, and a glass of beer. William had the same.

Henry turned a little serious. "How much money did you get out of father?"

"Not enough," William said, "but you know our 'survival of the fittest' father. I'm sure he thinks letting us struggle is an exercise in character building. Incidentally, he was thrilled that you are going with me. He gets us both out of his hair and can keep track of what we are doing with his money. He has friends in San Francisco who I know will keep him informed."

"I don't doubt it, but I appreciate his supporting us in this venture. I know he would like nothing better than for us to work in one of his businesses like George Jr. has, but he loves us enough to recognize that we need to make our own decisions and have our own experiences. That makes him a good father in my book," Henry said.

"He is a great father. But his choice of women is a little suspect. I think our stepmother likes me better than she does you, but I am sure if it were up to Susan she would not part with a dime for this venture."

"I have no idea why she dislikes me so much," Henry said. "Perhaps it is because she cannot control me and she knows it."

"None of us knows how to control you, Henry. It is part of your charm."

Henry laughed. "Thanks for the compliment. When do we leave for the City by the Bay?"

"I was thinking about a week from today. How does that work for your schedule?" William asked.

"That works fine. I am anxious to get out of Ohio and cannot wait to get to California."

"I have a reservation on the 10 a.m. Union Pacific and a sleeping car for two reserved. I assumed you would join me so I took the last one available."

"As I remember you snore loudly, but I will bring cotton," Henry joked.

"And I will remind you that I do not allow women in my car unless they smoke cigars and drink brandy."

"Is there any other kind these days? I will bring a good book. I am reading *Looking Backward* about a man who falls asleep and wakes up in the next century. I will lend it to you when I am finished."

"It sounds too intellectual for me. I mostly stick to newspapers," William said.

"I will pick up my ticket and meet you at the station an hour before departure," Henry replied.

The two brothers talked for nearly an hour about family matters and old times. Henry finally got up to leave and felt an urge to give his brother a hug, but instead leaned over and shook his hand.

After leaving William, Henry walked for several blocks; it was a beautiful day, and he had nothing else planned. He loved the smells of cooked sauerkraut and freshly baked bread from the surrounding shops. He passed several new clothing stores and a grocery that specialized in fresh produce.

Henry had soon walked off his excitement and took a horse trolley to the park near his home. The daffodils were in bloom, a sign that winter was over and spring was around the bend. New buds were sprouting on the trees, and the grass was getting greener by the minute.

HORSE POWER: Horse-drawn trolleys were a popular means of transportation in eastern cities in the 1880s.

He used his key to enter the front door. There was no need to bother the butler. He passed his father's study and heard someone call out, "Good afternoon, Henry." Seated in one his father's good leather chairs was Clarence Winters, his old fraternity brother at Harvard.

Winters stood up and walked over to shake Henry's outstretched hand. They both wore wide smiles.

"Clarence, my lad, what brings you all the way to Cincinnati?"

"Business, my man, business."

"What kind of business? I always thought you were an artist who was going live in Paris with some sweet thing on the Left Bank?" Henry teased.

"I am planning to paint again, but right now I have an opportunity that could mean never worrying about money again."

"What are you going to do, paint a masterpiece and sell it to the Louvre?"

"It has nothing to do with art. It has everything to do with gold," Winters replied.

Gold has always had the ability to pique a man's interest, but this was especially true after the great Gold Rush in California, where people made millions either discovering gold or exploiting the miners. It certainly sounded exciting to Henry, who was too impatient to make his fortune the way his father had—that is, investing, making good decisions, and watching his wealth grow over time.

Winters told Henry that he had met an engineering student named Ralph Bellows from Modesto, California, while at Harvard. Bellows was a fourth-year student at the Colorado School of Mines before enrolling in Harvard to earn a business degree. Over beers one evening, Bellows had told Winters about his father investing in the Lost Creek Gold Mine at the foot of the eastern Sierra Nevada near the small town of Bishop, California.

Bellows' father was a mining engineer and indicated major deposits of gold, lead, and silver had been discovered in the Lost Creek mine. The gold was very high quality, worth about $12 per ounce.

"His father thinks there is a fortune to be made in that mine," Winters told Henry. "His father used all of his savings and purchased the mine from its previous owners. I have come to you because my engineering friend and his father need capital to develop the mine. I desperately want to be a part of the venture. I know from our time together at Harvard that you are looking for a way to make your fortune. Since your father is an important banker and financier, I was hoping you would have some ideas for developing the mine. Perhaps you and your father would like to invest in part ownership?"

Henry listened intently to his friend's story, nearly hypnotized by the prospects. Making a fortune of his own had been his passion since he was a child. The thought of owning a prosperous gold mine appealed to his sense of romance as well as to his sense of entrepreneurship. He felt goose bumps all over his body.

As Henry listened, his eyes darted up to the beautiful woodwork of his father's bookshelves. He smelled the warmth of the leather of the chair he was sitting in and the faint smell of cigar smoke, his father's one real vice. As his friend finished speaking, Henry was silent as he let the goose bumps fall away. He thought clearly in the silence. There must be a way for him to become a part of the Lost Creek mine.

"Clarence, thank you for coming to me. I think the idea of developing a gold mine is fascinating, and it appeals to me a great deal. But I have to be honest. I have no serious money of my own, and next week I am leaving for San Francisco to open a store that sells safes. As you probably know, the stock market has been extremely volatile, and my father's bank, although solid, is taking a conservative outlook toward new loans. I doubt very much that I can interest him in financing a gold mine. But I would like to stay in contact should there come a time when I have the means."

"I appreciate your honesty, and I knew you would be interested," Winters said. "In the meantime, do you have any suggestions about how we could raise capital?"

"Have you thought about selling shares in the mine?" Henry asked.

"We have, but we are not sure how to go about it."

"I have a good friend who is a stock broker. He specializes in helping companies issue stock. I can give you his name and address, and I suggest you contact him while you are in Cincinnati." Henry took out the address book and notepad he kept in his coat pocket and the gold pen his father had given him on his 20th birthday, wrote down the broker's information, and handed it to Winters.

Winters stood and gathered his papers, placing them in a scruffy old briefcase. He was a tall man with a rather large build and a blond mustache above his generous mouth. He was tan from the sun, and although he was clean and well-groomed, his suit was old and his shoes worn. Despite his modest appearance, he seemed confident and knowledgeable, the kind of man you could trust.

After Winters left, Henry's thoughts turned to fantasies about how rich he could become if he owned the "Lost Mine of Bishop Creek." It was just the kind of get-rich-quick venture he had dreamed about.

Henry had no way of knowing that the Lost Creek Gold Mine would haunt his thoughts and dreams the rest of his life. Both a curse and a dream worth pursuing, it would influence every business decision he ever made and fuel every adventure, opportunity, disappointment, and success. If his life were a painting, the mine would be the background from which he would never escape.

San Francisco Bay – 1889 – Library of Congress – pencil sketch- artist unknown

CHAPTER 2
A Fresh Start

As William and Henry set out for San Francisco, they had two things in mind: starting a business and meeting the wealthy people who ran the city. The brothers were beyond excited to be making the journey, and the prospect of a trip on the nation's nascent cross-country train system was thrilling. The adventure had begun.

They traveled from Cincinnati to Kansas City on a railroad partially owned by their father, and then to Salt Lake City on the new Union Pacific line. They transferred trains at that point to the Central Pacific Railroad, another relatively new line. The Central Pacific took them through Sacramento, then to a port town called Alameda, where they would catch a ferry into San Francisco. They marveled that railways now tied the coasts. When the Union Pacific connected to the Central Pacific in 1869, it made history.

The train frequently traveled through mountain tunnels, darkening the cars' interiors for several minutes. At times the brothers could see the walls of solid rock, and they wondered how on earth the rail workers managed to get through mountains of solid rock. They later learned that Chinese laborers used picks and hammers to chip their way through, while the primarily Irish workers used dynamite and pneumatic drills. The brothers were amazed by the majesty of the Rocky Mountains and the Sierra Nevada, having never seen mountains that high. Though it was May, snow still covered the peaks framed by bright blue skies and lazy white clouds. Brightly colored wild flowers carpeted the meadows, and streams became raging rivers. Occasionally they would see deer or buffalo grazing or red-tailed hawks soaring overhead. Along the way were tiny villages in the distance and small cities where the train would stop to refuel.

The train cars were comfortable and nicely appointed with padded benches and curtains on the windows. Henry and William had first-class tickets that gave them access to a club car that served cocktails and beer at linen-covered tables. The club car became the dining car once the cocktail hour was over. The food was good and the servings were large. The view out the window often made eating superfluous to watching the landscape roll by. They found their fellow passengers to be well-dressed, educated, and friendly. Everyone seemed excited to go out West. Most had not been there before

Courtesy of California Pioneers Photo Collection

Commissary Car on the 1885 Union Pacific Railroad

When they arrived in the port city of Alameda, they saw three- and four-masted schooners and metal-sided ships anchored everywhere. One schooner was on its side with the masts leaning on the wharf. Thinking it must have tipped over, they were told the ship was merely "heaving down" so the bottom could be scraped for barnacles and other organisms. It was a cheap way to service your ship without taking it out of the water. They also saw a huge clipper ship, which was incredibly impressive with its multiple sails, huge masts, and pointed prow. They had seen pictures of the giant ships, but they were far more impressive in person.

The brothers were ushered to a large paddle-wheel steamboat called the Sacramento. These vessels could navigate shallow harbors and rivers more easily than deep-drafted sailing boats or steamships. The boat was large and comfortable. Although they had seen paddle steamers transporting goods from Cincinnati down the Ohio River to the Mississippi, they had never ridden on one before.

The Wilshire brothers were surprised by San Francisco's hilly landscape. Huge hilltop mansions could be seen from the deck of the ship, though they must have been a mile away. They knew the city was on a bay, and they could see a narrow ocean passageway shrouded in fog. They saw a small island someone said was Alcatraz, and another named Goat Island or Yerba Buena Island. What seemed like thousands of boats were anchored at the many wharves. The amount of activity was nearly overwhelming.

Painting by Lee of the Alameda about 1880

The steamboat unloaded them at the Pacific Mail Wharf, which was owned by the Pacific Mail Steamship Company, a venture of the Big Four railway magnates. They had heard the Big Four owned about half the city.

As they disembarked, they saw large horse-drawn wagons, streetcars, a few horseless carriages, and thousands of people milling about, tending horses, meeting people, or loading freight wagons. They noticed many Chinese with their long black pigtails and silky jackets. The smoke from the trains mixed with the smells of garlic and beef cooking over a wood fire. It was not Cincinnati, that was for sure. They could have used a cold beer, but there was not a bar in sight.

A handsome, well-dressed young man in a brown suit and bowler hat approached Henry and William. He was accompanied by a strikingly beautiful young woman in a blue dress and large hat. The man extended his hand and said warmly, "Henry, my man, wonderful to see you. We were thrilled to receive your letter and pleased at your decision to come to the City by the Bay. This must be your brother William the Strong." The young man turned and shook William's hand vigorously. The beautiful woman came forward and kissed Henry on the cheek.

Union Depot and Ferry House – San Francisco – 1885 -

This attractive young couple was John and Nora Peterson. Henry had met John in Paris two years before on the Grand Tour his father arranged after Henry's graduation from secondary school. John was also touring through Europe, and they became traveling companions and good friends. John's cousin had invited them to a birthday party when they were in London, where they were introduced to Nora Richardson and Agnes Phillips. John and Nora were surprised to learn that they were both from San Francisco but had never met, probably because their families had sent them to school in the East. They had spent little time in "The City," as it was called. The four spent a great deal of time together in London. Agnes was a wonderful conversationalist and talked easily to Henry about politics and the latest play in London they should see, but they lacked a romantic spark. On the other hand, it was obvious to anyone with eyes that Nora and John were attracted to each other. When they were together, there was no one else in the room. Henry was not surprised when John wrote six months later to tell of his engagement to Nora.

"How was your trip?" Nora asked.

"Amazing, simply amazing," Henry replied. "Seeing the buffaloes on the prairies after we left Salt Lake City was a highlight for me. The train was well-appointed, and our sleeping quarters were excellent. We enjoyed the entire trip."

"I loved the buffaloes as well—such magnificent beasts," she said. "What did you think of the tunnels through the mountains?"

"It is hard to believe that mere humans could carve such long tunnels through solid rock."

John said, "It just goes to show what 5,000 hungry Chinese workers can do. I understand that 5,000 Irishman did the same from the other direction."

"We had better claim our luggage before we get caught up," Henry said. "I would hate to lose our bags."

"Always the practical one and obviously correct," John said.

"Why don't you two get the luggage, and Nora and I will go get our buggies. You realize you are staying with us until you get your bearings?"

"That is very generous of you. We don't know one street from another, let alone the best hotels."

"We would not have it any other way," Nora said. "We have plenty of room, and you will enjoy the view. We will start showing you around tomorrow after you have rested."

"Nora, you are as charming as you are beautiful. I am glad this handsome rogue you married has not changed you."

"Change is not possible with Nora. The best you can do is soften the edges a little," John joked.

As they laughed, Henry could not take his eyes off Nora. She was one of the most beautiful women he had ever seen. He grudgingly joined William to claim their luggage.

John and Nora lived in Pacific Heights, a hilly area overlooking the bay and the city. It was a neighborhood of small, newly built Victorian homes, fashioned after the Queen Anne school of architecture. The neighborhood was colorful and picturesque, each house as charming as the next.

Example of a Queen Anne style of architecture –

Pacific Heights, San Francisco 1885

John and Nora's house was one of the most attractive, painted light blue with wooden gables, a circular corner tower, and a beautiful garden in front. It overlooked the bay, a large stand of trees, and a fort called the Presidio. It was a short walk from their home down to the harbor and a colorful shopping district. Henry and William were shown to their rooms. The house was not large but was comfortable for two people and guests. There were no servants. Once they were settled in, John invited them to join Nora and him in the sitting room.

Henry sat in a leather chair facing a large picture window with a view of the bay. "Nora, you and John have a lovely home. I love all the windows, and of course the views are stupendous."

"Thank you, Henry," Nora replied. "We built it four years ago and designed it ourselves with the help of an architect. You and William are our first real houseguests."

"We are honored," William replied. "What can you tell us about the city? We have read a great deal, but there is nothing like an insider's point of view."

"Where should I start?" John said. "I won't bore you with how the area was originally inhabited by small, loosely-knit tribes of Indians. Sir Francis Drake, the English sea captain, discovered the area in 1579, supposedly anchoring his ship, the Golden Hind, in the bay. I say supposedly because some doubting Thomases do not believe he ever landed here. Some say a Spaniard named Gaspar de Portola discovered the bay. Regardless, trading activities soon began between the Indians and the Spanish and later the Russians. It did not take long before the Indian population was decimated by the arrival of the white man. We see a few Indians in the city every now and then, but now they live mostly in the northern part of the state.

"Two hundred years after Drake and Portola, the Spanish built a series of missions up and down the state. The good fathers built the Mission San Francisco de Asis, later shortened to Mission San Francisco. The mission was built near a fort called the Presidio, which you can see from our living-room window. The Spanish were slow to develop the area, and by the time they got around to establishing themselves, San Francisco de Asis was overrun with English, French, Russian, and American explorers. Yankee fur traders discovered the otter and seal populations and came in droves. Whalers came into the bay on their way out to the whaling grounds of the Pacific. The Spanish owned large cattle ranches in the area and started to transport hides." John paused to sip from his wine glass.

"When Mexico became a country and won its independence from Spain in 1821, it allowed freer trade with outsiders and issued land grants up and down the state, but the Mexicans still had little interest in developing the area. From your history classes, you know about the Treaty of Guadalupe Hidalgo, where we acquired California from Mexico. You may also remember the Bear Flag Republic—a small group that revolted against Mexico and formed their own nation. There are streets near here named after various heroes of those days. Then came the Gold Rush, and everything changed.

"The men who came to California before the Gold Rush were a different breed. My father was among them. They were farmers, ranchers, and merchants for the most part. Most of the original American settlers were from the Deep South. You have probably heard of John C. Fremont, Jedediah Smith and Kit Carson who were among the first to settle here. Most people don't know that Andrew Jackson offered Mexico $500,000 for San Francisco Bay long before California became a state. Those Southerners knew a good thing when they saw it. Nora, why don't you jump in? I don't want to do all the talking. I am getting hoarse."

Nora smiled and her melodious voice sent chills through Henry as she spoke: "I would be happy to although you make a wonderful historian, John. I guess I can tell about one the most romantic periods of San Francisco history, the Gold Rush, and the miners who came with it. Gold was first discovered in John Sutter's mill at the foot of the High Sierra in 1848. Sutter should have become a millionaire, but he was a born loser and never really profited from the gold discovered on his property. When the word got out about 'gold in them thar hills,' people came west in droves. Thousands arrived expecting to find gold under every rock. Some came by horse and wagon; others came by ship around South America's Cape Horn. Many arrived by canoe, and some walked all the way. My father said that when he came to California in 1848 there were no more than 20,000 residents. A year later there were 100,000 people, all because of gold. Today, most people come either by train or, from the East Coast, by way of the straits of Nicaragua. I took that route once myself, and it was beautiful. But as Mark Twain said, 'Too many American-made billboards. It spoils the scenery.' "

To laughter, Nora continued: "People came from all over the world to mine for gold. The reality was that few people found any gold, or at least not enough to matter. The people who made money were the people who mined the miners. Shopkeepers, outfitters, and various kinds of entrepreneurs made millions supplying the miners with goods and services. Most of the miners went home, probably penniless, but those who stayed gave our city its international flare. There were whalers and Chinese, Italians and Germans, English and Russians, each with their own specialty. There were Russian furriers, Italian fisherman, German brewers, English bankers, and Irish bar owners. There were sailors from Australia, as rough a group as ever came to the new area.

"There were prostitutes galore of every shape and color. But there were also very refined people: musicians, actors, college professors, writers, doctors. Society was one of extremes, from well-to-do businessmen to ruffians, roustabouts, and crimps who shanghaied unsuspecting men into whaling boats for two-year shifts, stole people's money, and were not afraid to use violence to get what they wanted. I read the other day in the Sacramento Union that there were 1,600 murders recorded between 1860 and 1866, and only three men were ever convicted. That was twenty years ago, but some of that violence and coarseness still exist. Watch yourself when you walk around the harbor. Some of those crimps may still be lurking about looking to abduct crewmen."

William said, "I have read about the danger of being shanghaied in San Francisco, but I thought it was a joke. Besides, they would take one look at Henry and me and say, 'Not those two, they are too soft and too fat to be of any use.' "

"It is a safe city for the most part," John replied, "but there are areas where you need to watch your step. The Gold Rush brought a lot of thieves, prostitutes, and vagabonds, and they still frequent the areas around the Barbary Coast. That part of the city is fascinating, but don't go there alone. If you must go, you might want to take a policeman—or a revolver."

Nora added, "My advice is stay away from those areas. The food and music are not worth the risk of getting mugged. John, I hope you never frequent those areas."

"Of course not, my dear," John said, turning his head slightly and winking at Henry. "That is, unless there is an important reason to go there. I have been to the Barbary Coast a couple of times with business associates who want to see the sights. But we were in a large group and accompanied by a policeman. It pays to have connections."

Nora frowned. "You want to go to the girly shows. Be serious, John; it frightens me to death that you even think of going down there. Take your clients to the opera or something. You could get shot, beat up, or shanghaied. I am too young to become a widow."

"Sorry, my love, I should not have mentioned it. I promise not to take Henry and John."

Henry quickly changed the subject. "Where should we start looking for a store to rent and a place to live?"

"There are some nice rooming houses over by Telegraph Hill you might visit," John said. "The view is terrific, and the new cable cars make going downtown easy. As for storefronts, let me refer you to a friend in real estate."

Nora said, "I can be of assistance socially. We will introduce you to the most prestigious clubs in town to help you make contacts. It's a very cliquish city, and you need to establish yourselves with the right people."

"Nora, that would be wonderful," Henry said. "I have learned from my father that business is about who you know rather than what you know. Since I know so little about the safe and scale business, I will have to rely on making the right contacts."

"I think it is a little of both, Henry," his brother said. "I haven't told you yet, but I have already hired a couple of salesmen who know the safe and scale business backward and forward. They will teach us the ropes."

"William, you old fox, you are way ahead of me. I hope you see, John and Nora, what a challenge it will be keeping up with William."

"You are fortunate to have such a bright and handsome brother, Henry."

"You are making me blush, Nora," William said.

John and Nora served a wonderful red wine they said was made at a mission south of the city. Their hungry guests enjoyed the baked chicken covered in honey, small red potatoes, parsnips, and a salad that was particularly delicious. There were fresh raspberries and cream for dessert. The berries were like none the brothers had tasted, and Nora explained that California's weather was unparalleled for growing fruit and vegetables.

After dinner, cigars were offered. Instead of retreating to another room, Nora stayed and sipped a glass of sherry. This, too, was different than in the East.

Henry and William were eager to know more about the Big Four railroad magnates who owned much of San Francisco. "My father said the Big Four are a force to be reckoned with if we are to do business here," Henry said.

"Unless you are really big time, I don't think you have to worry about them," John said. "They are getting older, and although still formidable, they are looking at interests outside California and beyond railroads. As you know, they started the Central Pacific Railroad and connected it to the Union Pacific to make the transcontinental railroad. Of course, they were not interested in the railroad as an engineering challenge or as a patriotic duty. Their motivation was greed. They were getting $100 a mile of track and five acres of land on either side of the railroad. The fact of the matter is the transcontinental railroad was the idea of a man named Theodore Judah. He needed money to finance his idea, and the only people who would help were well-to-do Sacramento businessmen Collis P. Huntington and Mark Hopkins; a grocer, Leland Stanford; and a dry-goods merchant, Charles Crocker. A jeweler and another merchant initially joined the venture but later dropped out.

Charles Crocker   Leland Stanford

Collis P. Huntington   Mark Hopkins

"The Big Four were originally interested in selling goods to the mining companies on the other side of the mountains—to mine the miners, like Nora said. They soon pushed Judah out of the picture. When President Lincoln signed the Pacific Railroad

Act, it gave the Central Pacific and the Union Pacific generous land grants and subsidies to build the railroad. Central Pacific was to go east from Sacramento and Union Pacific west from Omaha, Nebraska. Good ol' Judah knew what he was talking about; the Big Four had hit the big time.

"Stanford took the contract as a cue, and ran for and won the governorship of California. The Big Four by now had various investors to finance construction. They issued contracts to a company they formed and began making millions—some of which went toward construction and some they kept for themselves. They viewed the actual building of the railroad as a minor pothole in the road to riches. The federal government became more enthusiastic about the railroad and increased its subsidies. The Big Four built in areas where they could maximize the subsidies. The state government saw opportunity and partnered with several counties to purchase $1.5 million of Central Pacific stock and a large number of bonds. That plus the federal subsidy allowed the Big Four to hire 10,000 Chinese workman and some skilled engineers to work under Crocker and connect the railroad in Utah. The Chinese accomplished amazing feats of construction with little more than wheelbarrows, picks, and loads of black powder."

William interjected, "We saw their work when we went through the tunnels on the train coming out. That is amazing, simply amazing."

Courtesy of Stanford University Special Collections

Connecting of Central Pacific
and the Union Pacific -May 1, 1869

"Right you are about that," John said. "The Central Pacific and the Union Pacific sometimes took some strange routes. Remember they got paid for every mile of track laid. The more track the more money. At one point they passed each other on different lines. If someone hadn't blown the whistle, there would be two transcontinental railroads instead of one."

Nora chimed in, "The Big Four did not stop with the transcontinental railroad. Once the Central Pacific was done, they began to build railroads all over California. They built a line from San Francisco north to Oregon and south through the San Joaquin Valley nearly to Los Angeles. They built smaller lines connecting railways all over the state, all with the blessing of the state Legislature. Sometimes called the Octopus because of their far-reaching tentacles, the Big Four owned the Legislature and the Supreme Court. They owned sixty acres of the waterfront where you arrived. They own the ferry that brought you here from Alameda. They own a shipping line called the Occidental and Oriental. They have a monopoly the size of which you cannot believe."

Henry thought of Andrew Carnegie as Nora spoke. He could feel his old anger at the trusts begin to churn in his stomach again. He thought to himself, "This kind of monopoly is morally wrong and should be stopped." Someday he would find a way to end it.

John said, "We are only telling you this because you asked and because you are going to go into business in this city. Their tentacles are everywhere, but there are many other very rich men here. The Big Four have other fish to fry elsewhere. Huntington, for instance, is now more interested in his Southern Pacific Railroad and in developing Los Angeles in a similar fashion as the Big Four did San Francisco."

Not immune to gossip, Nora said conspiratorially, "Mark Hopkins married a younger woman and paid the price. He was the best liked of the Big Four and a vegetarian who hated big houses. His wife didn't, and he gave her carte blanche to build the biggest house in San Francisco. It is up on a hill. You can see if for miles around."

"I think I saw it from the boat," Henry said.

Mark Hopkins Mansion – built in 1876 – destroyed by San Francisco earthquake

"You probably did. It isn't finished, but I can get you a tour. It is unbelievable. More like a castle than a house. Hopkins died several years ago without having set foot inside."

"Funny how that happens," William said. "The wife builds the house; the man provides the dough and dies before seeing the house completed."

"Charles Crocker also has a mansion on Nob Hill," John said. "It is my favorite. He is busy now building a mansion in New York City. But he is not well; he has diabetes. Stanford also has a large mansion on the hill. He is campaigning for U.S. senator. You will see his signs all over the city. Rumor has it that he has made a lot of bad investments and is hurting for money. Huntington hates him and fights with him about taking money out of the railroad. In any case, you need to see the mansions of Nob Hill. They are a sight to behold."

"We would love to take a tour," William said. "You know, Henry is becoming somewhat of a socialist, so that kind of wealth sickens him. I, on the other hand, view it as inspirational. Where can I get mine, and more important, when?"

Laughing, John replied, "Well, there is plenty of opportunity in California. You have come to the right place. There are a lot of very wealthy folks in the city, and you need to meet some of them as soon as possible. I understand you both went to Harvard, and there is an active Harvard Club in town. There is also a Merchant's Club you definitely want to join. One of you could become a Mason, and the other might want to join the Bohemian Club. Henry, you like artists and writers, as I recall; maybe the Bohemian Club is for you."

"The Bohemian Club sounds good," Henry said. "Nora, could you set up an introduction for me?"

"If the Masons don't care that I drink and am not especially religious, I guess I could join for the sake of the business," William added.

For the next week, John and Nora showed their two visitors around town and introduced them to a real estate broker, two boardinghouse keepers, several of their friends, and some of the best restaurants in town. Cable cars were being installed on several streets, and it was almost as much fun as an amusement park to ride the ones already operating. They were shown the mansions on Nob Hill and the beautiful Palace Hotel, easily the largest and grandest hotel they had ever seen.

The Palace Hotel – 1887 – one of the grandest hotels in America

They toured Cow Hollow, an area near Pacific Heights, with its new buildings and neighborhoods. They went down to the Embarcadero and saw the numerous wharves that gave the streets their names: Lombard Street Pier; Union Street Pier; Broadway Street Pier; Jackson Street Pier, and Washington Street Pier, just to name a few. Hundreds of ships were moored at the piers, from three-masted schooners, whaling ships, and military vessels, to Italian fishing boats called feluccas and Chinese junks that were primarily shrimp boats. There were saloons everywhere to serve a diverse clientele that included uniformed sailors, disheveled Australian seamen, and oyster-men who looked like they could eat nails for dinner.

In contrast, farther south of the Embarcadero was a completely different waterfront. A yacht harbor sheltered beautiful boats, and beautiful people strolled around the area. There was also the Alaska Oil Wharf, where large oceangoing ships waited in line for fuel. There was the California Sugar Refinery, and the Union Iron Works wharf next to the Pacific Rolling Mill, where the smell and heat transported Henry back to Newport Pipe and Cable. All the wharves seemed to converge at Market Street, which was close to the waterfront but led to banks, insurance companies, stock brokerages, and large hotels.

A week after their arrival, the two men settled into a modest rooming house near Telegraph Hill with separate living quarters for each. It had a fabulous view of the harbor and was a short walk down a steep wooden stairway to the Embarcadero. They also rented a good-sized store on Sacramento Street near Front Street, close to the major banks and many of the clubs they soon joined with John's sponsorship. They both applied for membership in the Harvard Club, open to those who had attended for a year or more, so Henry qualified. William applied for membership in the Masons and Henry in the Bohemian Club. And they both hoped to become members of the Merchants' Club.

They used their father's contacts and began filling orders from Eastern companies for safes and scales of various sizes and shapes. They also scoped out the competition, pretending to be customers as they visited showrooms. There was Dynamic Safe Company, which had a large outlet and would be a major competitor. Then there was Reynolds' Scale, an established company with a major store in town. The brothers had business cards and stationery printed and found a printer that specialized in sales brochures. They met with the two salesmen William had hired and found them to be charming and knowledgeable. They spent days visiting manufacturers and began to plan the layout of their store. The inventory, coming by train from the East Coast, would arrive in about a week. They tried to use the time wisely, and when their inventory was delivered, they already had several orders from friends and acquaintances.

Thanks to their father's many contacts, they were accepted into the clubs they had chosen. The Harvard Club in San Francisco was founded in 1874, one of the first such clubs in the country. It proved to be a little stuffy, but the members would make valuable contacts. The Bohemian Club, composed of journalists, artists, and musicians as well as businessmen, accepted Henry. He had a special affinity for the journalists, who talked in depth about nearly every topic imaginable. Two university presidents and several military officers were also members. Henry George, the author of the single tax ideology that Henry was introduced to in Anatolia, Ohio, was a member. A drinking club called the Jolly Corks was associated with the organization, and although Henry was not a big drinker, he found their company very entertaining. The Merchants' Club accepted them both, and John, who was also member, introduced them around. It was easily the best club for business contacts since networking was the members' primary goal. It was several months before William was admitted to the Masons, and he had to endure an initiation process that he deemed ridiculous. But he found plenty of drinking buddies and enjoyed the experience overall.

Their friendship with John and Nora earned the two young bachelors invitations to a number of parties hosted by the city's social elite. Nora's father was a city councilman and owned a large stock brokerage. John's father was part owner of the Bank of

California. An excellent dancer and conversationalist, Henry quickly became popular. He had the ability to ask challenging questions without coming across as rude, and he was a good listener with the ability to remember details about the people he met. Both brothers had a good sense of humor and good looks, which appealed to the female bonnes vivantes. A good horseman, Henry often took early morning rides in a beautiful wooded area not far from the Presidio. He suggested to many of his new friends that it would make a wonderful park. He even had a name for it: Golden Gate Park for its proximity to the entrance of the bay.

Henry became acquainted with some of the city's leading politicians. The brothers were warned to steer clear of the Chinese, whose immigration was controversial. An Irishman named Denis Kearney had led an effort the previous year that resulted in Congress passing the Chinese Exclusion Act. A Chinese laundry owner in town was challenging the law, and as a result all Chinese laundries in the city were being boycotted by the townspeople. The Wilshires liked clean shirts but wisely found other places to have their laundry done. Politically, the city was divided between the interests of the Big Four and the big banks, and those of the small farmers, ranchers, and fisher-men. Henry's sympathy for the working class made him root for the little guy, but he kept those views to himself in social situations. Still, labor unions were coming into their own in California, and Henry secretly attended several meetings of the sailors and warehousemen unions. The tone of those gatherings suggested a class conflict in the making, Henry thought. He could see it coming.

As accepting as John and Nora's friends were of Henry and William, the men still felt like outsiders. San Francisco was a relatively new city, but still cliquish. And it suffered the same separation between the wealthy and the workingman that existed in the East.

Among the wealthy elite was William Henry Crocker, a member of the Yale Club, which sometimes held mixers with the Harvard Club. A handsome, elegant man with a closely trimmed beard and mustache, he founded the Crocker National Bank, made himself president, and became a major downtown developer, including building the Palace Hotel. Crocker started a telegraph and telephone company, a major insurance company, and a gas and electric company. He was perhaps the most powerful and important man in San Francisco—and a major snob. Henry got to know him well. They were about the same age and from wealthy families, and Henry watched how the man conducted himself. An enthusiast of art and new inventions, Crocker was self-assured without being arrogant. He limited his inner circle to the social elite with the exception of titled foreigners. Crocker never invited Henry into his home but was friendly toward him.

Another young man to watch was Patrick Calhoun, a corporate attorney, real estate investor, and grandson of South Carolina politician John C. Calhoun. Patrick, who was also interested in railroads, was among the new young elite of San Francisco. William met Patrick at a bar and they became friendly. Patrick even invited William to his home to meet his wife.

The women of San Francisco were another force to contend with. Some of the most important women had inherited fortunes from their rich husbands. Everyone knew of the immense fortune Mark Hopkins had left his wife, Mary Sherwood, who was twenty years younger. It was her idea to build a huge mansion on Nob Hill with large towers and intricate gingerbread trim. There were lots of rumors and even a newspaper article or two about her affair with her designer. When Hopkins died suddenly of a stroke, she began openly seeing her designer paramour, causing more coverage and somewhat of a scandal. She eventually left the Bay Area and built a huge home on New York's Eighth Avenue.

There was also Sarah Althea Henry, their host at several cocktail parties. She was a beautiful charmer in her thirties, married to Senator Alfred Sharon, "The King of the Comstock" and one of the richest men in San Francisco. The marriage was supposed to be a secret. She did not know he had a mistress named Gertie Dietz who had borne his child. Sharon rented a lavish apartment at the Palace Hotel for Sarah and unbeknownst to her, kept another one for Gertie across the land bridge at the Grand Hotel. Rumor had it that the senator was worn out from walking back and forth across the bridge. In the end, Sharon divorced Sarah and paid her $25,000 a month. He later regretted the amount and filed to annul the marriage, ending the need for the alimony. Sarah appealed the decision with her new husband, David Terry, a former California Supreme Court justice, and Judge Stephen Fields ruled against them. About a year later, Terry met Fields on the train to Sacramento. They had words, Terry slapped Fields, and Fields' bodyguard shot Terry dead.

Henry met Sarah at a reception Nora held one evening. Perhaps her mystery was part of the attraction, but Henry viewed Sarah as a woman to be admired. There were many women like that in the city. Kind of like the Barbary Coast in a dress. You needed to be careful.

Like Sarah, the Barbara Coast was an attractive nuisance. Despite Nora's admonitions, Henry and William had to see it for themselves. They had met a police lieutenant who had offered to show them the sights. It was a hot summer night when they made the excursion into the fascinating but dangerous area north of Chinatown.

Lieutenant Murphy was dressed in civilian clothing, but the bulge of his pistol was visible beneath his light coat. He was over six feet tall and wore a bowler that made him seem even taller. His size seemed to challenge people as they walked down the street. The first thing that struck the brothers was the smell, a mixture of stale beer, urine, and sauerkraut. There was also the shocking array of prostitutes in costumes that ranged from dance-hall girls to geishas with silk Chinese skirts slit at the thigh. Despite their provocative dress, the women were less than attractive. Smelling of sweat, most were plain, many were missing teeth, and a few had pockmarks on their faces. The Chinese prostitutes were sometimes an exception, and Henry thought many of them were quite beautiful. Thin, with long black braids and dark eyes, they wore loose pants of blue or black, and their nipples were visible through the thin silk of their blouses.

Bars were plentiful with as many as ten in a block, and large burly men guarded the entrances. Music wafted from the drinking establishments: player pianos clinking out ragtime and even some Gilbert and Sullivan tunes. Chinese porters or "coolies" walked the streets swinging bamboo poles with heavy baskets tied to the ends. As they walked, the brothers noticed handmade street signs on cross streets. The real street names were covered and in their place were monikers like Murderer's Alley, China Alley and Stouts Alley. The bars were also colorfully titled. There was the Cock of the Walk, the Star of the Union, the Roaring Gimlet, and Bull's Run, to name just a few. Some of the bars were also gambling houses. Their police friend took the lead and walked into one that he knew. He told them to watch their pockets and watches.

As they entered, a man carefully scrutinized each of them and said, "Be watchful, lads. We don't want any New York sharpies or disguised policeman in here. We play an honest game here, and we are proud of it." Henry wondered if the man knew Murphy was a cop. They walked into a long room full of tables and dealers dressed in long black robes and wire masks that partially hid their features. They heard the sounds of coins hitting the table and the clicking of a faro wheel turning past pictures of one-, five-, and twenty-dollar bills, and they saw players reluctantly draw money from their pockets to play again. Six gullible men were trying to spot the hidden queen as a three-card monte hustler changed the card's position so quickly that the eye could not hope to follow. Most guessed wrong, but some guessed right, keeping the others interested. Other patrons were playing five-card draw on a table covered with chips. The air was so filled with the smoke of cheap cigars smoke that it hurt to take a breath. Some men were drinking beer at the long bar where nude paintings hung over a mirror behind the bartender.

At that moment, a fight broke out at the poker table, and one man pulled a knife. In a flash, the doorman grabbed the hand holding the knife, bent it back to a painful angle, and pushed the player's nose into the table. The man screamed in pain, and the knife dropped to the floor. The doorman lifted him by his collar, effortlessly carried him to the entrance, and threw him out the door. No one seemed alarmed, and the noise that had paused for a moment returned as the players went back to their games, the beer drinkers to their glasses and the piano player to his tune. So this is the Barbary Coast, Henry thought.

Deciding it was an opportune time to leave, the men made for the exit. A short, fat woman bumped into Henry, and he felt a hand reach into his breast pocket. He quickly grabbed the outside of his coat where his wallet was located and pushed the woman away. "Hey, Molly, is that you?" Murphy said to the woman. "I thought you moved to Monterey. I suggest you walk away before I run you in."

Henry noticed that Molly had no teeth. She looked at Murphy, cursed him under her whiskey breath, and staggered away.

"I am glad you warned us about thieves. She might have made off with my wallet," Henry said.

"Most of them are clumsy fools, too drunk to be skilled at picking someone's pocket. Those at the railway terminal are much better at it. Even I have to be careful there. So have you seen enough?"

They had seen enough of the Barbary Coast but decided to walk through nearby Chinatown, strolling along Sacramento Street to Kearny. Murphy told them many of the Chinese originally came from the Guangdong province to work in the gold mines. They were met with suspicion and prejudice by the other miners, and many returned to San Francisco or went to work building the railroads. The Chinese Exclusion Act of 1882 forbade them from owning property, voting, marrying outside their race, or testifying against a white man in court.

Library of Congress – Dover classics in public domain- Arnold Genthe photo

Early street scene of Chinatown - 1885

Murphy explained the different occupational groups: The Hock Kay men were barbers, the See Yup men were primarily laborers, and the Sam Yup men were merchants. A See Yup man was not allowed to compete with a Sam Yup man. And the Chinese would only do business with Sam Yups, avoiding white-owned shops. There were benevolent associations known as the Six Companies, which cared for all the people who lived in Chinatown and tried to discourage prostitution. There were also "tongs" to which every man must belong. The tongs, which originally offered legal services and loans but eventually turned to crime, offered their members protection from other tongs and occasionally from whites.

Murphy said the Chinese loved to gamble but they avoided the Barbary Coast and stuck to their local Chinese gambling houses. They mostly played fan-tan and lottery games. Murphy said the Chinese did not own revolvers or guns but kept sharp razors or hatchets as weapons. He said he had never been as frightened as when an angry Chinese man charged him with a hatchet.

The smells in Chinatown were wonderful, though unidentifiable to Henry and William. Chinatown, unlike the Barbary Coast, was clean, colorful, and seemingly safe. Both visitors thought that if you wanted to show someone the sights this was a better place to go. There was lots of foreign-sounding chatter going on but nothing hostile despite their being the only whites on the street. Interesting shops offered silk and ivory carvings and wooden bowls. At one store, Henry purchased a Buddha carved from ivory, and William bought a silk scarf. Despite all the anti-Chinese sentiment in San Francisco, Henry decided he liked the people and the culture and found it much more enjoyable than the crass, crude Barbara Coast. He was glad he saw it but not sure he wanted to return. Chinatown, on the other hand, was a place to visit again and again.

As Henry was getting to know the city, he was also growing increasingly familiar with its wealthy denizens. At a dinner party Nora had for her father, Henry met a lovely woman named Arlene Ivers, the daughter of Dennis Ivers, a lawyer and respected businessman. She was taller than Henry and had been educated at Wellesley College, one of the new women's colleges in the East. Arlene was knowledgeable about politics, history, art, theatre, and economics. She was friendly, honest, and gracious, and Henry enjoyed her company immensely, although there were no romantic sparks between them. The time they spent together was filled with laughter, lively debate, and youthful enthusiasm for new ideas. Arlene was not a socialist, but she knew the writings of Karl Marx and how some of his thinking was influencing American labor unions. She agreed that the labor theory of value had merit, but she was against the redistribution of wealth. Henry talked about Henry George's single tax and told her that George was a member of the Bohemian Club. He had met George at a dinner party, and they had had a long conversation.

One Sunday Henry invited Arlene to go riding with him. She was a better rider than Henry was and would gently tease him about it. She agreed go riding despite his inferior skill and they set out on a beautiful summer morning the following Sunday.

The day was so lovely that they decided to ride all the way out past the Presidio to where the new Golden Gate Park was being built. It was rough terrain, but they were both good riders who took the long rough ride as a challenge. Arlene lived not far from John and Nora but in a much larger home.

The horses were kept in stables not far from the Presidio. Henry hired a buggy to pick up Arlene and take them to the stables. When she came to the door, he complimented her on her striking appearance. She wore a long black riding dress and a stylish black hat to match. Her riding boots were polished, and her hair was drawn back into a bun. She was not a beautiful woman, but she was definitely attractive. Henry had purchased new riding clothes and a wonderful pair of brown leather riding boots, but he felt dowdy in contrast to Arlene.

"Arlene, you look as pretty as a picture in those riding clothes. I should have brought a camera."

"You don't look so bad yourself. Aren't we the stylish ones?"

"You never know who we might see on the trail. It pays to look your best."

"That is just like you, Henry, always looking for an opportunity to impress someone."

"Time is a-wasting. Let's get started down to the stables," Henry said, ignoring her barb.

They took the buggy down to the stables and got their horses. Arlene's horse was a spirited black Arabian stallion, a large animal with a gleaming black coat and a long tail. Arabian horses are a beautiful breed, versatile, strong, and capable of both speed and endurance. The black beauty had been in Arlene's family for ten years and was a favorite. Henry rented a brown and white Appaloosa. Appaloosas are known for their speed and are often bred for the racetrack. Henry's horse belonged to a friend from the Merchants' Club.

Henry understood there were certain rules of etiquette to be observed when a man went riding with a woman. Before allowing a woman to mount a horse, a man should inspect the saddle and bridle to be sure all is secure. A stableman had likely already done a thorough inspection, but the point was to demonstrate concern for the lady's safety. It was then the gentleman's province to assist her in mounting. While he holds the horse, the lady, with her skirt in her left hand, grabs the pommel of the saddle with her right hand, her face turned toward the horse's head. Facing her, the gentleman stands at the horse's shoulder, stoops, and allows the woman to place her left foot in his right hand. She then springs up, and he lifts her gently into her seat, allowing her to place her left foot in the stirrup and arrange her riding habit. The gentleman stays in place until she is settled and has the whip in her hand. In dismounting, the gentleman takes the lady's left hand in his right, removes the stirrup and takes her foot in his left hand, lowering her gently to the ground.

Early 1885 drawing showing proper riding attire

Henry and Arlene performed this ritual perfectly and set out on a path that climbed up a steep hill. A half-hour later, they stopped to look down on the hundreds of ships docked at the harbor's piers. Most impressive were the large clipper ships with their magnificent masts. One clipper ship was coming into the harbor; with its full sails, it looked like a picture Henry had once seen. There were two metal government warships, Chinese junks, and Italian *feluccas*. The fog that typically shrouded the bay had lifted, giving them a view of Alcatraz Island and Goat Island as well as the Golden Gate isthmus. It was a picturesque scene, and they lingered for at least twenty minutes.

"All right, Henry, enough of this sightseeing. We came here to ride, so let's get to it."

Arlene's stallion took off as if someone has touched its hind-quarters with a hot iron. It ran down a rough path and below some pine trees. Henry spurred his horse and galloped after them.

As Henry got closer, he saw a large wildcat come out of no-where and dart across Arlene's path. The horse reared up and, with Arlene hanging on for dear life, began running blindly. Arlene tried to control the beast, but it was too frightened to obey. Henry realized the horse was headed toward the cliffs that yielded to a beach below and knew he must cut off the horse and rider before they reached the edge. Henry dug the spurs attached to his new boots into the side of the appaloosa, which galloped hard after the stallion.

Henry guided his horse at an angle he hoped would inter-cept Arlene's horse. Leaping fallen logs, dodging hanging limbs, and skirting large boulders, horse and rider sidled up to the wild-eyed stallion. Henry had no idea he could ride that well or that the horse could run that fast. Perhaps the appaloosa sensed what he was trying to do.

Henry reached out with his right hand and grabbed the stal-lion's bridle, pulling gently to bring it to a stop. Both horses were covered with frothy sweat and breathing hard, as were the riders. Arlene was sobbing, and Henry dismounted to help her down when the stallion reared up and clawed the air. One hoof clipped Henry's jaw, and he fell to the ground. Arlene screamed as blood began streaming from his face. He did not want to alarm Arlene, but he was dizzy and could not seem to get to his feet.

Fortunately, they weren't alone. Two other riders had seen the wildcat scare Arlene's mount and were just seconds behind

Henry, arriving as the stallion struck Henry in the face. One immediately went to help Henry and the other to help the fragile Arlene down from her horse. The man told her how fortunate she was because her horse was heading for a cliff with a hundred-foot drop to the beach. This was not a wise thing to say to woman nearly in a state of shock. Arlene fainted dead away, and the guilty man lowered her to the grass.

The man at Henry's side saw a six-inch gash in Henry's jaw. A former soldier, he knew how to stop the bleeding. He took out his handkerchief and began placing pressure on the wound. He noticed Henry had lost a tooth and was bleeding from his mouth as well. Henry was pale and close to going into shock. By then other riders had gathered, and one was a physician who took charge until a vehicle could be found to take Henry and Arlene to a hospital.

Henry spent two days at the hospital. Though his injuries did not appear to be serious, the doctor wanted to be certain he was all right. Arlene, who had been examined and released, spent hours at Henry's side, telling him what a hero he was and how she would never forget what he had done. Her grateful father also came to visit, pledging to return the favor in any way possible—a promise Henry would call upon in the years to come. He and Arlene remained friends for many years. She went on to marry the son of Pierpont Morgan and move to New York City. As a result of the accident, Henry had a long scar on his chin and grew a beard to hide it. The beard changed shape now and again, but he wore a Van Dyke for most his life.

After word of Henry's heroics spread, Arlene's friends and family made it a point to give Henry their business, and Wilshire Safe and Scale thrived. But after two years, it became stale for the two young entrepreneurs. The business was stable, but it would take years of conservative practices to make any real money. Fortunately, Reynolds Safe Company saw their small store as competition and offered to buy the brothers out. The Wilshires feigned lack of interest, the competitor raised its bid, and the brothers made over $100,000 profit on their original investment. Their father was pleased at their astute business acumen.

Meanwhile, Henry had heard that land speculators were making millions down in Los Angeles. There were tales of people buying a lot for $500 in the morning and selling it for twice as much in the afternoon. Not only was the weather beautiful but a courageous investor could also make a great deal of money quickly. Of course, this was exactly what Henry wanted to hear. At the same time, he received a letter from his friend Clarence saying that he and his father had found some backers for the Lost Creek Gold Mine and that things were progressing nicely. Although Henry thought the mine was still the best investment he had come across, he decided a gold mine was riskier than real estate. He wrote to Clarence to say he was still interested and to keep him informed.

As Henry packed up his belongings and said goodbye to John and Nora, he thought of the important experience he had gained in San Francisco. He had engaged in a profitable business venture, learned the importance of knowing the right people when starting a business venture, and made some important and even powerful friends. He also discovered that he and William were a good pair. William's easy handshake and outgoing manner were the perfect complement to Henry's more introspective and refined personality. Henry also realized that the sailors, Chinese, shipbuilders, and oystermen he had encountered had only fueled the working-class sympathies he had developed in Ohio. Perhaps most important, Henry had learned that he had the gumption and ambition to make things happen. Los Angeles offered a challenge that he gladly accepted. Henry could not wait to get at it.

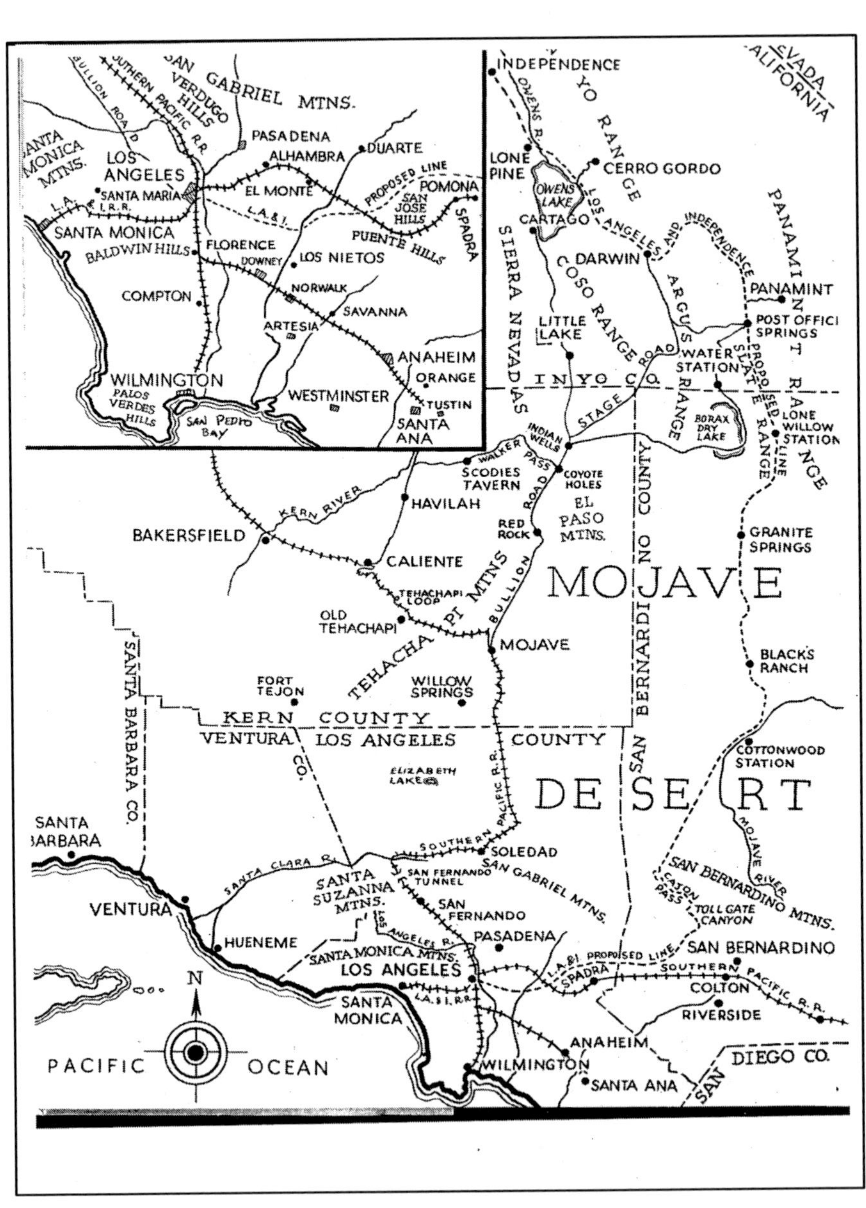

SAN GABRIEL MTNS.
VERDUGO HILLS
SANTA MONICA MTNS.
BULLION ROAD
SOUTHERN PACIFIC R.R.
PASADENA
ALHAMBRA
DUARTE
LOS ANGELES
SANTA MARIA
EL MONTE
PROPOSED LINE
POMONA
SAN JOSE HILLS
SPADRA
L.A. & I.
L.A. T.L.R.R.
SANTA MONICA
FLORENCE
PUENTE HILLS
BALDWIN HILLS
DOWNEY
LOS NIETOS
COMPTON
NORWALK
SAVANNA
ARTESIA
ANAHEIM
ORANGE
WILMINGTON
WESTMINSTER
TUSTIN
PALOS VERDES HILLS
SAN PEDRO BAY
SANTA ANA
INDEPENDENCE
NEVADA
CALIFORNIA
OWENS R.
INYO RANGE
LONE PINE
CERRO GORDO
OWENS LAKE
CARTAGO
LOS ANGELES AND INDEPENDENCE
PANAMINT RANGE
DARWIN
ARGUS RANGE
PANAMINT
SIERRA NEVADAS
COSO RANGE
POST OFFICE SPRINGS
LITTLE LAKE
STAGE ROAD
WATER STATION
SLATE
INYO CO.
BORAX DRY LAKE
LONE WILLOW STATION
INDIAN WELLS
WALKER PASS
PROPOSED LINE
SCODIES TAVERN
COYOTE HOLES
KERN RIVER
HAVILAH
EL PASO MTNS.
SAN BERNARDINO COUNTY
RED ROCK
GRANITE SPRINGS
BAKERSFIELD
CALIENTE
BULLION ROAD
MOJAVE
TEHACHAPI LOOP
TEHACHAPI MTNS
OLD TEHACHAPI
MOJAVE
BLACK'S RANCH
FORT TEJON
WILLOW SPRINGS
KERN COUNTY
VENTURA
LOS ANGELES
COUNTY
COTTONWOOD STATION
SANTA BARBARA CO.
ELIZABETH LAKE
DESERT
SOUTHERN PACIFIC R.R.
SAN BERNARDINO MTNS.
MOJAVE RIVER
SANTA BARBARA
SANTA CLARA R.
SOUTHERN
SOLEDAD
SAN FERNANDO TUNNEL
SAN GABRIEL MTNS.
SAN BERNARDINO
CAJON PASS
TOLL GATE CANYON
VENTURA
SANTA SUZANNA MTNS.
SAN FERNANDO
HUENEME
SANTA MONICA MTNS.
LOS ANGELES R.
PASADENA
L.A. & I. PROPOSED LINE
SPADRA
SAN BERNARDINO
SOUTHERN PACIFIC R.R.
LOS ANGELES
L.A. & I. R.R.
COLTON
RIVERSIDE
SANTA MONICA
ANAHEIM
N
WILMINGTON
SANTA ANA
SAN DIEGO CO.
PACIFIC OCEAN
SAN

CHAPTER 3
City Planners Paradise

It was a cold November day in 1886 when the Wilshire brothers left San Francisco and headed south on the Southern Pacific Railroad. The views as they left the Bay Area were spectacular, and the vineyards that had been harvested a few months before were all changing color. Splashes of orange and red leaves and brilliant green vines turned the canvas of rolling hills into a brightly colored landscape dotted with spreading live oak trees. This was the California they had imagined during long, dreary Eastern winters.

They stopped at a train station in Stockton, the third-largest city in the state, and continued south through Modesto, Visalia, and Bakersfield. They much preferred the coastal areas to the dry interior of the state, where there were cattle and sheep ranches and little else. Leaving Bakersfield, the train began to ascend and loop around. If a train were long enough, the engineer would be able to see the caboose below as the track turned back upon itself. The brothers were told this was the Tehachapi Loop, designed to help the train power up a steep grade. They arrived at another desert town called Mojave and finally at their destination Los Angeles.

When Henry left San Francisco, Nora had given him an excellent history of California to read on the train by O.P. Fitzgerald. Called *California Sketches*, it was a popular book of short stories about early California. The book contained brief biographies of leading Californians past and present. He found the book great company on the train ride and kept it as a reference for many years.

Henry had already learned from John and Nora about the Franciscan fathers building a series of twenty-one missions up and down the state. Now he was discovering how the Yang-na Indians had settled around the Los Angeles River. Los Angeles itself was founded in 1781 by forty-four *pobladores,* or townspeople: Spaniards, Indians, blacks, and Californios of mixed race. The Indians had beaten a path to the nearby tar pits, gathering the goo to use in making baskets. In search of roofing materials, the settlers followed the Yang-na trail to *la brea*—"the tar" in Spanish—establishing El Camino Viejo ("the Old Road").

The new settlement was named El Pueblo de Nuestra Senora la Reia de Los Angeles—the Town of Our Lady of the Queen of the Angels—appropriate for such a heavenly area. In 1784 the Spanish governor of Alta California granted the first ranchos, each to an important Spanish soldier to use as he saw fit.

When Mexico won its independence from Spain in 1821, the Mexicans were too busy to worry much about Alta California. The area continued to grow, and Los Angeles became a stopping point for all travelers headed north. It was also a place for mountain men, Indians, and outlaws. When war broke out between the United States and Mexico in 1847, the Los Angeles area was all but forgotten. When the Treaty of Guadalupe Hidalgo ended the war in 1848, it meant the old Spanish rancho system was defunct, and the old families quickly sold their land to the highest bidder before it was taken from them.

Courtesy Henry Huntington Library Special Collections
Don Pio Pico – the last Mexican governor of California

The bust of the Gold Rush brought many disappointed miners and Chinese to Los Angeles. Some continued mining in the desert areas of the Mojave. Many took advantage of the climate and fertile soil to raise cattle and grow citrus and other crops. Others were former merchants who decided to return to their previous professions. Lawyers, doctors, dentists, barbers, and a wide variety of storekeepers opened their doors during the period from 1850 to 1870. Despite the onslaught of civilization, Los Angeles was still a rough place, including Chinatown's Nigger Alley, where it was said there was a murder a day.

In the 1860s, drought killed thousands of cattle, sheep, and horses, and land was often sold for taxes. The large ranchos were sold off and divided into small ranches where water was available; the discovery of artesian wells in some areas rescued many ranchers and farmers. But the death of an estimated 50,000 head of livestock forced Southern California's largest landowner, Abel Stearns, to mortgage most of his ranchland in 1868, which was purchased at a sheriff's sale and eventually sold to a land development company.

Stearns had hired lawyer Robert M. Widney to subdivide his property, and Widney had accepted land in lieu of a fee. The lawyer decided land was more profitable than lawyering, so he bought a small printing press and started the monthly *Los Angeles Real Estate Advertiser* in 1869. Thanks to Widney and others, word got out that Southern California was a land of milk and honey, and people arrived by the thousands. It was standing room only on steamships from San Francisco, and hundreds of wagons from all directions could be seen on the roads headed toward Los Angeles. The city became a boom town.

When the Big Four completed the Southern Pacific Railroad extension between Los Angeles and San Francisco in 1876, the region changed forever. But it came at no small cost. The powerful foursome told the Los Angeles city fathers that they would have to pay $602,000 if they wanted Los Angeles instead of San Diego to be the railroad's final freight destination. The Angelenos were irate and tried to start their own railroad. In the end, the Big Four used violence, bribery, and sabotage to destroy the opposition, and the city fathers were forced to pay the tribute.

Library of Congress Photo
Los Angeles begins to look more modern - Street scene -1880

Of course, the Southern Pacific, though the biggest, was not the only railroad in Los Angeles. Nevada Senator John P. Jones founded the Los Angeles and Independence Railroad in 1875 to connect his Panamint mines in Inyo County to the Santa Monica Bay. Jones bought an interest in the San Vicente Rancho from Colonel Robert Baker, and the two laid out the new city of Santa Monica. Jones, who built a large home and bathhouse, urged people to come to the beach for their health and enjoyment. They did—in droves. Soon other beach cities were established, and the coast was thriving. Though the mining operation went bust a few years later, the railroad extended all the way to downtown Los Angeles.

Arcadia Hotel and Bathhouse — Santa Monica - 1880

The Board of Trade, the precursor to the Chamber of Commerce, began sending thousands of pamphlets to the East and South and running advertisements in newspapers and magazines extolling the glories of Southern California: There was no snow and little rain. There were flowers and fruit trees growing wild, and the beauties of nature were unbelievable. You could enjoy the mountains, the desert, and the ocean in the same day. Land was cheap, and banks were eager to lend to farmers, ranchers, and investors.

But late in 1875 a financial panic derailed the land boom. Temple and Workman's bank failed, and Workman put a bullet through his head. Jones was eventually forced to sell the Los Angeles and Independence Railroad to the Southern Pacific.

The Board of Trade did not give up and in 1881 invited the California Editorial Association to hold its annual convention in their city. They succeeded in persuading—or perhaps bribing— the newspapermen to sing the praises of Los Angeles' perfect weather and inexpensive land.

In 1881 the Southern Pacific Railroad completed a line between Los Angeles and San Francisco, and in 1885 the Santa Fe Railroad opened its competing line. People were coming to the new city in droves. Most of the new arrivals were American born, many came from the Middle West, and a large proportion were people of some means. Prosperous Midwestern farmers turned their holdings over to their children and moved out west. Many sought a warmer climate to retire. Some came to speculate in land or other business ventures.

William Wolfskill, a land developer, had bought a large section of the old Rancho San Jose de Buenos Ayres in 1884 for $10 per acre. He later sold it for ten times what he had paid for it after collecting a judgment of $293,000 from the railroad in a right-of-way dispute and setting up eight hundred lots for the town of Sunset. Investors bought and sold quickly, and money changed hands so rapidly it was difficult to know who owned what. A savvy dry goods merchant named Isaias W. Hellman, who had arrived from Bavaria in 1859, started the Farmers and Merchants Bank in 1872. Governor Richard Downey also saw the need for a bank, so he started one, ignoring any conflict of interest. Francis P. F. Temple and John Workman also opened a bank. Loans were plentiful and offered at a low interest rate. Farmers and ranchers could borrow as long as they owned property or livestock for collateral.

A major boost came in 1885, when the Big Four connected the transcontinental railroad with the Santa Fe. Los Angeles now had two railroads heading to the sea, one connecting with San Francisco, another heading east and third heading south. There was also Jones' Los Angeles and Independence Railroad. The Big Four were losing interest in the West and had split up as a powerful cabal. Collis P. Huntington was the only one who still had interest in the Los Angeles area. He worked with his nephew Henry E. Huntington on the Southern Pacific Transportation Company. In 1898 Henry purchased the narrow gauge Los Angeles Railway and built a huge home on a large estate ten miles east of Los Angeles. The Angelenos realized that to attract new residents they had to spruce up their city.

During the 1880s a number of inventions would help make Los Angeles seem like a modern city. Electric trolley cars, incandescent light bulbs, cash registers, electric arc welding, steam turbines, and electric furnaces were changing how people lived and worked. Telephones were available to those who could afford them. The automobile and the pneumatic tire were gaining popularity, but most roads in Los Angeles were not paved, so horses and buggies were still better suited to the terrain. There was the new Nadeau Hotel, which was four stories high and had electric lights, telephone service, and an elevator—the only one in Southern California. A cathedral built in 1876 had become the focal point for the downtown area.

A plethora of stores small and large opened along the new avenues of Los Angeles Street, Main, and Spring, and an opera house and more retail were planned for Broadway Avenue. There were dry goods stores, groceries, clothing stores, and jewelry shops. There were stationery shops, bakeries, hotels, banks, restaurants, saloons, barbershops, and, of course, real estate offices.

Courtesy of the Huntington Library Special Photo Collections

The City Hall and Jail in 1880 with Escrow Indians standing in wait for new customers

The city was home to a Wells Fargo Express Office and two newspapers, The *Star* and *The Express*. There were sidewalks

91

built of wood and curbs of stone on some streets. A park was established right in the middle of town, and electric lights were installed on the major streets. Eucalyptus, pepper, sycamore, and orange trees were planted along the curbs. The smell of freshly cut lumber was everywhere.

New neighborhoods were springing up as well. The grand old houses on Bunker Hill looked down on the developing city below. Boyle Heights just across the river attracted many wealthy landowners and merchants. Wolfskill Real Estate continued to sell lots in an area called Beverly Wood. New towns sprang up to the east and south: Santa Ana, Tustin, Newport, Cucamonga, Pasadena, San Fernando, Downey, Norwalk, Garden Grove, Orange, Anaheim, Alhambra, Ontario, Pomona, Claremont, Arcadia, and Sierra Madre. The homes were different than those in the east. They often had large lots, fences, surrounded by landscaped lawns and isolated from business activities. Orange groves appeared and trees were everywhere. In some of the new towns there were grand homes made of brick and stone. In some areas there were ranch homes and sprawling wooden residences with bay windows, balconies, porches and high pitched roofs. There were still some of the old adobe houses left over from earlier days, which were still cool in summer, warm in winter, and earthquake-proof.

In 1885 the Santa Fe Railroad decided to compete more directly with the Southern Pacific and started a fare war. A ticket to the Mississippi Valley dropped from $125 to $95. The fares continued to drop until finally you could buy a ticket from

Kansas City to Los Angeles for $1. People arrived from the East in droves—along with real estate investors.

Courtesy Huntington Library Special Collections
Los Angeles/Spring Street from First Street, 1885

Real estate offices opened in storefronts and even on sidewalks. Agents, often called Escrow Indians by the populace, became a nuisance to some established businessmen. The Escrow Indians had left their ethics on the other side of the Sierra Nevada, and false contracts and downright hoodwinking increased in proportion to the amount of money involved. They often sold land they had not seen to short-term investors who would sell it the next day to some other sucker.

The Escrow Indians hired flatcars to take people out to tracts of land, where they provided free lunches, brass bands, and all the beer you could drink. In this circus-like atmosphere, some people were making thousands of dollars. In the mid-1880s, like most bubbles, this one came to an end. Land prices were inflated far beyond what the properties were worth. The banks refused to lend money unless the land was in town or the applicant put at least 40 percent down. This tight credit brought investment to a halt. The Escrow Indians lost their shirts—at least on paper. As one said, "I have lost half a million dollars in a week. The sad part is $500 of it was in cash." Investors and real estate agents who had been barbers, lawyers, dentists, and barkeeps returned to their previous occupations. Los Angeles returned to sanity.

The land boom of the 1880s was actually a good thing for Los Angeles. The publicity had exposed Easterners to talk of the region's beauty, weather, and vitality. Maybe they couldn't make a fortune there, but they could certainly go for a visit.

Henry put down his book as the train approached Los Angeles. He may have missed the land boom, but that didn't preclude long-term, legitimate investments in real estate and businesses, he thought to himself. Henry and William were met by their sister Clara and her husband, Charles C. Carpenter. They had arrived from Ohio the previous week to see for themselves if the stories about Southern California were true.

When Henry and William got off the train at the Los Angeles and San Pedro Railroad station at Alameda and Commercial Streets, they were struck by the noise and dust. The roads outside the rustic station were compressed dirt, the smell of horse manure lingered in the air, and dogs were running about. People were shouting for what few rental buggies there were. It was complete chaos, and Henry briefly considered getting back on the train for San Francisco. Charles had rented a large buggy that seated four. Henry swallowed hard, and the brothers located their luggage and climbed aboard.

Courtesy of the Huntington Library Special Collection
Finally a Real Station - Station Arcade Depot - 1888

They traveled from the station to the Nadeau Hotel on the corner of First and Spring streets. The streets were narrow and made of packed dirt rather than asphalt. There were horse trolleys and buggies and a few horseless carriages. Mansions perched on a hill overlooking the city. There were hundreds of small shops along the streets and what looked to be offices of various types above the storefronts. The buildings were just one or two stories high, probably because the area was prone to earthquakes, they surmised. The city was larger than they had imagined and was obviously growing.

The Nadeau Hotel was the first four-story building in Southern California. Some people called it "Nadeau's Folly" because it was so big and so far south. It was nothing compared to the

Palace Hotel in San Francisco, but it was new, shiny, and clean. The travelers were met by dapper bellmen who helped Clara down from the carriage and took their luggage into the hotel. The large lobby had red velvet on the walls and redwood counters where the guests registered. An array of green plants gave the lobby a certain charm. Next to the lobby was a large, noisy bar that was filled to capacity.

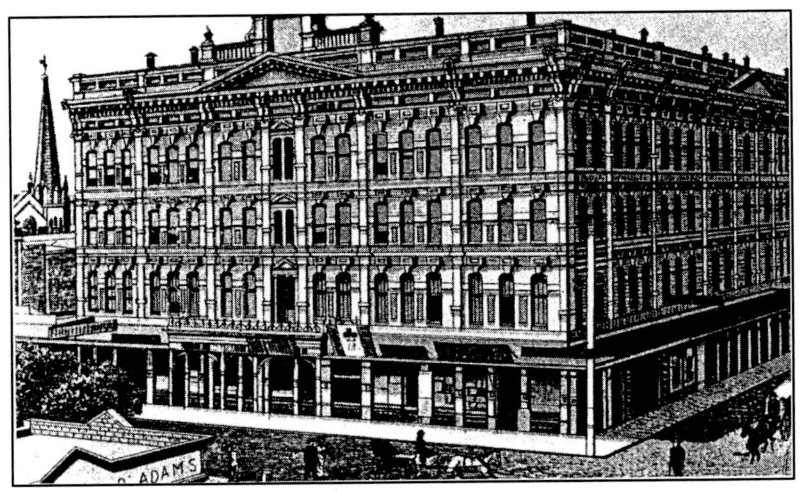

Nadeau Hotel – 1887 – Remi Nadeau spent $236,761 to build the hotel, which was considered a huge sum.

They checked in and were given adjoining rooms. The hotel had few vacancies, and they were glad they had made reservations. Their rooms were spacious with large bathtubs and four-poster beds. You could hear the bells of the trolleys and other street noise, but closing the windows muffled the sound. William suggested they clean up and meet in the bar. Dirty from the long train ride, everyone readily agreed.

Now refreshed, the travelers reconvened in the well-appointed bar. William had arrived first and already had a beer in hand. Once they were all comfortably seated at a large round table, Charles asked Henry what he thought. "Is Los Angeles what you expected?"

"Like San Francisco, it is still a little rough, but that is to be expected in a city that is just coming into its own," Henry said.

"I agree," William chimed in. "I liked what I saw. Construction everywhere, well-dressed women, lots of saloons. The bartender told me the Philadelphia Brew House is making the best beer anywhere, so I had him pour me a glass. It is stupendous. Kind of a nutty flavor with a touch of wheat."

Charles replied, "Beer is beer to me. Some is yellow and some is brown. I prefer wine or scotch."

"You are talking sacrilege to your brother-in-law," Henry teased. "He prides himself on his taste for the suds."

Clara had been taking in the surroundings and asked, "Henry, who are those men yelling at people like circus barkers?"

"I assume they are holdovers from the real estate hawkers who made thousands of dollars selling cheap land to Easterners and San Franciscans. Their ethics were dubious, and we have been warned by friends to steer clear of them. The truth is the land boom is pretty much over, but there are still conservative, stable investments to be made."

William disappeared toward the bar for refills while Henry talked about his plans. "I have a number of things I want to do today. My friend John recommended a banker at the Farmers and Merchants Bank, where I will open an account. He also gave me the name of a legitimate real estate broker whom his bank uses. I don't know if you two are interested in investing, but if you are, you might want to go with me."

"I am not sure we should invest," Clara said. "This place looks a little rough to me. Perhaps we will let you get the lay of the land first."

"That is fine, but remember Cincinnati looked like this once. Cities take time to develop. Potential is what I want to see," Henry said.

Charles asked, "How do you know that you are not buying at the top of the market?"

"You don't. It is a gamble to be sure," Henry said. "But it is not my intent to buy property and turn it over quickly. I am interested in acquiring a good piece of land and sitting on it until the city spreads out to meet my property. I have given this some serious thought. If I can determine which way the city will grow and buy undeveloped land for a good price, I will surely make a handsome profit in the end."

"Henry you are sounding increasingly like father every day," Clara said.

Just then, William returned with a tray of four beers and a stranger in tow. "Look who I found at the bar—a fellow Ohioan. This chap is from Toledo. He has been investing in real estate for the last six months and has a few tips for us. Jake, meet my sister, Clara, her husband, Charles, and my charming brother Henry."

Henry said, "Pleased to meet you, Jake. I am always glad to meet a man from Ohio."

Jake shook hands all around. He was a big man with thin gray hair, a rumpled suit, mud-splattered white spats, and a large red nose that suggested he was a drinking man's drinking man.

"Howdy, folks. Welcome to Los Angeles. Are you here for your health, for the weather, or for the chance to make some money?"

"A little of each," William responded. "How long have you been here?"

"I have lived here about a year, working in real estate. Business was great about a year ago, but it is harder now. Be careful whom you listen to when it comes to investing. There are many unscrupulous brokers out there who will sell you land that does not exist. I don't buy land unless I see it and the bank approves the contract."

Clara said, "That sounds like a reasonable approach. How does one get started in this investing business?"

"You need someone who knows the territory," Jake said. "Someone who knows what is valuable and what is a scam. I hate to brag, but I think I match that description."

William said, "What kinds of properties are you representing, Jake?"

"It just so happens that today I bought a piece of land out in Pasadena that is surrounded by orange trees and has a beautiful view of the mountains. The former owner was an old man who can no longer irrigate the groves in the summer and cannot afford to hire help. I bought it cheap. If you are interested, I would be glad to show it to you."

Henry said, "We appreciate that, Jake, but we have just arrived. We need to get our bearings and settle in. Give us your business card, and if the property is still available next week, we might want to take a look."

Jake reached into his pocket for a business card and handed it to William. "Don't wait too long. This property will not last. I am taking a potential buyer there this afternoon."

Before leaving the four to their beer, Jake shook hands again and took note of the diamond ring on Henry's finger and the diamond stickpin on his lapel. As Jake walked away, William said, "Seems like a nice chap. I hope we are not making a mistake by not going to see his Pasadena orchard."

"I think Henry was right," Clara said. "We just got here, and although Jake seemed like a good sort, you never know."

Clara and Charles left the bar to go walk around town. She was eager to visit some of the dress shops she had seen along Spring Street.

Henry and William went to look for the Farmers and Merchants Bank, which the bellman said was on Fifth Street just a few blocks away. They walked along the street and were struck by the well-dressed people. The men could have been from Chicago and the women from New York. They did not expect to see cowboys and Indians, but they did think the people would be less sophisticated than they appeared.

The brothers passed several stores with tables out front and apparent hucksters pulling people off the street to show them photos and drawings of properties for sale. Pictures were plastered on storefront windows, and signs advertising properties were everywhere. One of the "realtor offices" had a brass trio playing and free candy for the children. People were rushing about the tables, and a few were writing checks. It was obvious that business dealings were energetic, but Henry found the pace uncomfortable and obnoxious. He knew these men were hanging on to a time that was long past.

They found the Farmers and Merchants Bank on Main and Commercial Streets. The bank was founded in 1871 by Isaias W. Hellman. The bank appeared businesslike and modest by Eastern bank standards. It was a two-story building. They asked the receptionist if they could see Ralph Morgan, the manager. The receptionist showed them to a large office toward the back of the large room.

Framers and Merchants Bank on Main and Commercial Streets in 1885.

The receptionist introduced them, and the brothers gave the banker their business cards and said they were friends of John

Peterson. The manager said he knew John well and asked how he and Nora were getting on. There was much small talk about San Francisco and what brought Henry and William to Los Angeles. Henry explained their desire to buy a property on the outskirts of town and hold it until the city expanded. Morgan praised their level-headedness in contrast to the quick-deal shenanigans taking place on the street. He said the latest scam was brokers selling repossessed agricultural property. A buyer would not discover that a property lacked clear title until after he had given the broker a large down payment. The broker would then feign ignorance, say he had been cheated by the seller, and walk away with the deposit.

Henry and William looked at each other and thought of Jake. That was a business card they would throw away. The Wilshires opened an account with the bank and established a line of credit. They had money from the sale of their safe and scale business plus some additional funds their father had wired them to invest on his behalf.

It did not take long for Henry and William to take advantage of the contacts they had been given by their San Francisco friends. Henry was particularly interested in a nascent organization that was not unlike the Harvard Club in San Francisco. The California Club would be exclusively for professionals, with a strict dress code and short-term room rentals for guests. It would locate near the downtown area on Figueroa Street. The California Club would prove to be a great asset to Henry Wilshire. He met many key leaders of Los Angeles at the club, including banker Isaias Hellman, an influential lawyer named

Henry W. O'Melveny, successful land developer Abbott Kinney, and Harrison Gray Otis, who led the Los Angeles Daily Times.

Henry told banker Morgan about his interest in real estate, and Morgan recommended a thirty-five-acre abandoned barley field on the western end of the city. It was a wedge-shaped plot that smelled of the oil being pumped from the wells in the distance. The western end bordered Sunset Park, a brown, weed-infested piece of land that was anything but a park. Henry learned that the owner was a widow who had deeded the land to the city. The western end of their parcel was much better because it bordered on Westlake Park, the city's pride and joy. Westlake Park had a manmade lake, beautiful walking trails, and lush landscaping. It was a gorgeous green space. Henry learned it was just a twenty-mile horseback ride to the ocean. The $52,000 price was right, and the Wilshires purchased the property with the intent of holding it until the city expanded west.

Security Pacific National Bank Collection/Los Angeles Public Library
Westlake Park around 1886 – showing homes
along the shoreline in the distance

As their network expanded, Henry and William heard that the new land of opportunity was in Long Beach, about thirty miles south of Los Angeles. There was a potential harbor there, and if the railroad extended its line to the water, property values would increase many times over. Henry always believed that when one door closed, another door opened. In this case the door that had closed in Los Angeles was opening in Long Beach. The Wilshires visited and immediately saw its potential. They found rooms in the Long Beach Hotel and rented an office on the ground floor. The hotel was a short walk from the small downtown area and the beach.

Courtesy Long Beach Library Historical and Special Collections
**Long Beach Hotel- Wilshire offices were on the first floor-
originally called Hotel Wilmore**

Henry found he had a talent for city planning. He loved predicting where a city would develop, where future streets should be built, and what they should look like. He was not a surveyor or an engineer, but he had never let a lack of credentials stop him. He began mapping out the city of Long Beach, which would incorporate in 1888. He named one long, wide thoroughfare Pier Boulevard and another Pine Street, which he envisioned as a broad avenue leading to the ocean.

Security Pacific National Bank Collection/Los Angeles Public Library
Pine Street of Long Beach –Widened according to Wilshire's plans

Henry made sketches and put trees and lampposts along his roads. He showed the sketches to several city leaders. His enthusiasm was catching, and he was asked to make a presentation. They were so impressed that they asked the city engineer to take Henry's sketches and develop the street plans accordingly.

Henry saw that Long Beach was a natural place for a harbor, but the bays and estuaries were not deep enough for large vessels.

That could be solved by dredging, as he had seen in San Francisco and Oakland. He realized the small Rattlesnake Island at the entrance to the harbor could serve as both a defensive position and a gateway. If the harbor could be developed and someone could persuade a railroad magnate to extend a line from Los Angeles to the Long Beach harbor, the city would develop rapidly, and investors could make a fortune. He floated this idea to city leaders, who liked the concept. Henry and William approached the Los Angeles County Board of Supervisors, which granted them the right of way if they could find a railroad to build it. Henry wanted to call it the Southern Pacific Alameda Line and hoped he would have an opportunity to present the plan to Collis P. Huntington. He had no idea that Collis P. had plans of his own for developing a harbor for Los Angeles.

Henry and William lived at the Long Beach Hotel for nearly a year. They liked the small town and its access to the sea. As always, Henry was interested in the area's history, and he spent hours talking to the old-timers who stayed at the hotel.

***

Henry learned that Long Beach was developed by John Temple and Abel Stearns—names he recognized from reading about Los Angeles history. Temple had bought part of Rancho los Cerritos for $3,025 in 1842. Stearns purchased Rancho los Alamitos between Los Angeles and the harbor for $6,000 in 1843. Both cattle ranchers had taken Mexican brides; Stearns married a beautiful sixteen-year-old named Arcadia Bandini, and Temple wed Rafaela Cota, whose family had owned the rancho.

The powerful ranchers employed a small army of workmen, equestrians, and ex-soldiers. When the war with Mexico started in 1845, U.S. troops landed in San Pedro harbor and claimed it for the United States. Stearns and Temple would not be overrun by what they considered a foreign army, so they fought back. Their cowboys and ranch hands defeated the American army at the battle of Rancho Dominguez. But the victory was short-lived; the Treaty of Guadalupe Hidalgo ended the conflicts in California, and the large ranchos became part of California Territory.

When California became a state in 1850, it attracted an entirely new group of businessmen and entrepreneurs. Temple and Stearns were landed gentry, but it was Phineas Banning who bought land along the harbor, naming the city he founded there after his hometown of Wilmington, Delaware.

The Civil War came in 1861, and there were concerns about the loyalty and security of the Los Angeles area because of the many Southern transplants. Governor John Downey pledged support to the Union and ordered the arrest of Confederate sympathizers. Banning deeded much of his property to the Union Army for a fort on Rattlesnake Island, where Camp Drum was established.

After the Civil War, Temple decided to retire after successive years of severe flooding, drought and thousands of cattle deaths ate into the ranch's profits. Lewellyn Bixby and his cousins Thomas and Benjamin Flint bought Rancho los Cerritos from Temple for $20,000 in 1866 and appointed Jotham Bixby to manage the new sheep ranch. Jotham Bixby became known as the father of Long Beach but it was his cousin John W. Bixby who named the streets, established parks and most importantly established the oceanfront area.

Around the same time, other small towns were springing up nearby. In 1865, Governor Downey founded what would become his namesake city, planting orange groves and pioneering the modern subdivision. In 1867 a wagon master named Griffith Dickenson Compton led a small group of pioneers from Stockton to the area that would be named after him. Downey also established a link with the Butterfield Stage Line from St. Louis to his town, calling the line the Imperial Highway.

The stage line brought hundreds of people to the area much like the railroad brought thousands to Los Angeles. The influx of people began a land boom, and prices skyrocketed. A large hotel was built right on the beach, and tourists and health seekers came in droves.

Everything was going well for the Wilshire brothers until 1889, when the Long Beach Hotel burned to the ground and many of their dreams went up in smoke along with it. The land bubble burned out about the same time as the hotel. As had happened in Los Angeles, Long Beach investors owed more on their properties than they were worth. Fortunately, the Wilshires had not invested too heavily in land, and they moved on to greener pastures.

Just south of Long Beach was the newly incorporated Orange County, where many land investors and potential citrus growers went after the Los Angeles land boom. People who originally came to Los Angeles discovered Orange County's rolling hills, fresh sea air, and ready water supply. They found that orange, lemon, walnut, and almond trees thrived there. A great market existed for citrus and nuts if growers could find a cheap way to transport the crops. If they only had a railroad line.

Henry and William rented a small cabin in an unincorporated area in Orange County not too far from the Anaheim River. Investors often hung out at a nearby restaurant, and one evening at dinner the brothers overheard two men discussing a real estate venture with a third man who looked like he did not belong in Orange County. The well-dressed Easterner was heavily bearded and had a long, dark mustache. Henry overheard him say, "There is little doubt that the area would benefit from a railroad, but I question whether some ranches and a few groves produce enough to justify a line."

The two men he was meeting with were young, blond, and handsome. The taller of the two said, "Please excuse me, Mr. Fullerton, but I think you underestimate the area. My brother Edward and I have a large grove in Sierra Madre not too far from here, but it lacks a good source of water. In contrast, this area has a fine river nearby, and the soil is excellent for growing citrus." The second young man, Edward, interjected, "George and I came from a family of Massachusetts merchants and knew nothing about farming when we arrived. But now we realize this is an area of great opportunity. We believe Orange County will be the next Los Angeles, but for the area to develop, it must have a rail line. As you know my brother and I purchased 430 acres of land just north of the town of Anaheim. We also own more acreage south of town. We know that that your railway, the California Central Railroad, is a subsidiary of the Santa Fe Railway and you are looking for a right of way to the south. We are prepared to give your railway a half-interest in our land if your railway right of way includes a proposed site for a town. We are also prepared to name the town after you a railroad official, as a sign of our goodwill."

"You Amerige brothers have impressed everyone in the area with your enthusiasm and hard work," the older man said. "If anyone could succeed here, it would be you two. However, I am afraid you have your work cut out convincing me that the Santa Fe should build a rail line through Orange County to San Diego rather than further inland."

Henry could not resist interrupting. "Please forgive me for butting in, but my name is Henry Wilshire, and this is my brother William. We hope to invest in this area, and I want to assure you, Mr. Fullerton, that there are many more like us who see the value of Orange County. As in Los Angeles, Long Beach real estate has gone sour. The future is in Orange County."

The older man laughed and said, "You young men are ganging up on me. What kind of experience do you bring to land development, Mr. Wilshire?"

"I own a thirty-five-acre plot west of Los Angeles and recently helped design the layout of the city of Long Beach. I am certain members of the City Council will vouch for my skill and foresight."

"It just so happens the mayor is a friend of mine. I will inquire about you if you don't mind. I am familiar with the Amerige brothers here, and they have impeccable credentials. Perhaps you two sets of brothers would be a good team."

Edward said, "There is always room for new investors. Perhaps we can discuss our mutual interests at a later time. At this juncture, Mr. Fullerton, can we be assured that the Santa Fe Railroad will consider our proposal? We will secure the right of way if the railroad agrees to run the track next to the site we think would make an excellent town. Perhaps we could name it after you, Mr. Fullerton."

"I see you are appealing to my sense of vanity, Edward. That is not really necessary, but the railroad officers would hardly object to a town named after its chief railroad agent."

Henry sensed brilliance at work. He suspected the Ameriges owned much of the land where the railroad would locate. And they probably owned the land where the town would be developed. How clever to offer the land for a rail line and then name the town after the chief railroad agent. Henry was not certain it would work, but it had lots of appeal.

The railroad agent and the Amerige brothers said their goodbyes, and Fullerton promised to get back to them in a week.

Courtesy of Local History Room -Fullerton Public Library
George Fullerton –Railroad Agent

Courtesy of Local History Room Fullerton Public Library
Edward and George Amerige
Founders of the city of Fullerton

Henry and William waited until the Ameriges returned to their table and then approached them.

"Please excuse our intrusion, gentlemen," Henry said. "Interrupting your conversation was most impolite."

"Not at all, gentlemen, not at all," Edward replied. "You were a little presumptuous, but your support for our plan may have helped swing Fullerton over to our way of thinking."

William said, "I admire your persuasiveness. I assume you own the property where the railroad and the town would travel?"

"Is it that obvious?" George said with a smirk. "Well, George Fullerton is a savvy businessman. He no doubt knew that from the start. It should not affect his willingness to route a line through our property if he thinks it will benefit the railroad."

"Could I be even more presumptuous and ask if we can invest as well, either purchasing property from you or in the area where you think the railroad would travel?"

"It just so happens we are short on cash at the moment," George replied. "We own about 400 acres just south of here in addition to the land we are proposing for a town. The land is along the river where the railroad is likely to go. It could also be used for ranching. Are you interested?"

"We are definitely interested," William said. "When can we see the property?"

Edward said, "How about tomorrow? Where are you staying? We will pick you up and show you around."

A week later Fullerton notified the Ameriges that the railroad had accepted their offer. He would meet with them in two weeks to discuss the route. The Ameriges informed the Wilshires of their success and said their offer to sell the 400 acres still stood. After some negotiation, the Wilshires became part owners of what would become the town of Fullerton.

Over the next six months the Amerige brothers implemented their plan. The Santa Fe Railway would pass through Fullerton en route to San Diego. Henry laid out the town, designing a wide street he called Commonwealth Avenue and Wilshire Park, named for his father, in the middle of town.

Courtesy of Fullerton Public Library
Wilshire supposedly laid out this corner of Commonwealth Ave.
His store is pictured in the building on the right.

Courtesy of Fullerton Public Library
Photo of building Wilshires built and where their Land and Real
Estate Office was located. They may have lived upstairs.
This photo was taken about 1895 after they sold the building.

The Wilshires started a land development company, the Fullerton Land & Trust Company, as did the Amerige brothers. They were friendly rivals. The Ameriges were more committed to the area and stayed for many years. The Wilshires stayed only a few years but kept some of their orchards for much longer.

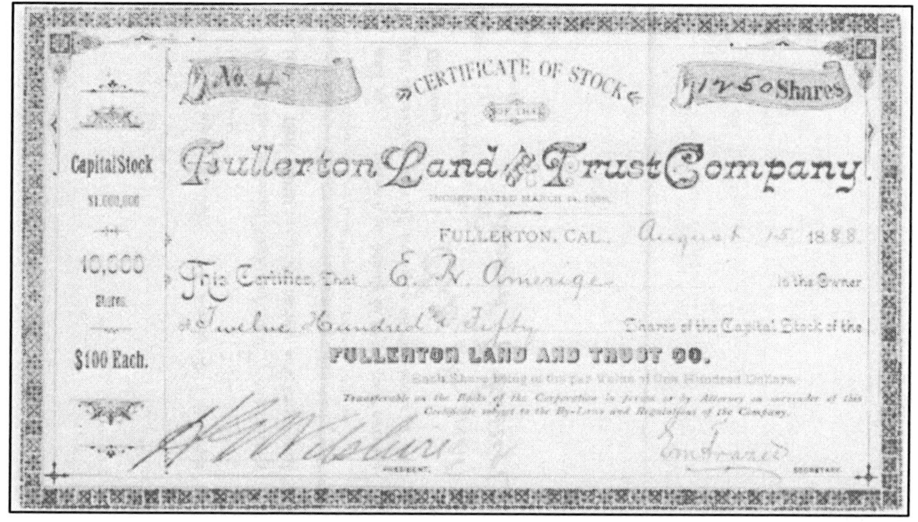

Copy of stock certificate courtesy of Scripophily.com
Fullerton Land Certificate showing exchange of stock between Wilshire and Edward Amerige

The citrus industry expanded a year later when Charles Chapman, a major citrus grower, developed the Valencia orange. The variety traveled well and, combined with Parker Earle's refrigerated railcar, made transporting oranges and lemons to the East Coast more reliable and profitable—even more profitable in the long run than the oil that was discovered near Fullerton in 1891.

Security Pacific National Bank Collection/Los Angeles Public Library
Drawing of early citrus groves in Orange County

Henry and William were content as orchard owners, but they never lost touch with their Los Angeles contacts. Henry still attended many California Club social activities and met an attractive Welsh woman named Hannah Owen at one of their dinners. Hannah had long brown hair, beautiful green eyes, and a good figure. She was also a socialist whose views were much more radical than Henry's. She believed violence was the only way to deal with the greedy owners of the trusts. William did not like the feisty Hannah, but Henry was in love. She had a young daughter from a previous marriage, but that did not dissuade Henry. They married in 1889. William moved back to San Francisco.

In 1890, their father died and left nearly everything to his second spouse, Sarah, who disliked Henry. Henry received only a small inheritance and later challenged the will. Henry claimed that Sarah was mentally unstable, but his case was laughed out of court. She eventually gave Henry $200,000 to shut him up.

Henry was becoming increasingly enamored with socialist ideas. He was particularly influenced by Edward Bellamy's book *Looking Backward.* It was about a young man, Julian West, who fell asleep in 1887 and woke up in the year 2000. The United States had been transformed into a socialist utopia, and the West character told of stores filled with every kind of merchandise imaginable and of consumers receiving credit based on their productiveness. People worked just six hours per day and retired at 45. Public kitchens fed people free of charge, and no one went without medical care. The goods of society were equally distributed, and criminals were treated as mentally ill. Two judges tried every case, and disagreement meant the case must be retried. Education was free to all, and no one was without a job. It was a creative book that accurately predicted many things to come.

Early copy of famous Bellamy novel

Henry was also influenced by Hannah. Ann anarchist, she believed all governments were corrupt. The only answer was to shoot the leaders and transfer power directly to the people. Henry still believed in democracy and capitalism; voters just needed to elect those who would champion socialist ideals and causes. Henry attended several socialist meetings in Los Angeles and found he liked giving speeches about his ideas. He was a decent orator, and people listened. They cheered his ideas and praised him for holding such populist views despite his wealth. They even gave him a nickname, the Millionaire Socialist, because he often gave speeches dressed in a tuxedo. He was hardly a millionaire but liked the nickname and used it often in his brochures and publications.

In 1890 the Socialist Labor Party decided it was time to run a socialist for Congress. Party members selected Henry as their candidate in the Sixth Congressional District, making him the first socialist to run for national office in the United States. He received fewer than 200 votes, but that was not the point. The campaign proved that a socialist could run for office, and it advanced socialist causes in the public forum.

When he came to Los Angeles, Henry had joined The Scribes, a club for journalists and authors. The Bohemian Club in San Francisco had introduced him to a number of writers, and he had enjoyed the intellectual interaction. The Scribes allowed him to return to the world of journalists, novelists, political theorists, and poets. Henry liked to write almost as much as he liked to play golf and give speeches. After his father's death, he used part of his inheritance to start *The Weekly*

Nationalist. The paper was sent mostly to party members. It lost money, but Henry knew it would.

After two years of marriage, Hannah decided she did not like life in Southern California. Orange County was beautiful but unsophisticated. She longed to return to London and its educated, well-read people. She begged Henry to take her back to Europe, and Henry finally conceded. He scrapped the newspaper, hired a caretaker for his groves, and bought tickets for his small family to New York, where they planned a stopover on their way to London. Both had friends in New York, and it was where the socialist cause had begun. They wanted to be exposed to the latest ideology. The decision would set the stage for things to come.

Henry Gaylord Wilshire about age 39

CHAPTER 4
New York City and London

As Henry got off the train at Grand Central Depot, it occurred to him that some cities make you feel more alive. New York City was one of them. The high-rise buildings, well-dressed people, and sound of horses' hooves on the asphalt reminded you that you were in an unusual place. New York City in 1891 was one of the most populated cities in the world—and one of the most exciting. Because the New York Central Railroad tracks were so close to the New Haven tracks, it was easy for your luggage to get lost in the chaos. Plans were being made to build a much larger station called Grand Central Station, but that was a decade away. Henry found a skilled porter who located their luggage easily.

Norfolk and Hester Streets, New York City, 1898

Henry, Hannah, and Hannah's nine-year-old daughter, Dora, were staying at the Gilsey House Hotel at Broadway and 29th Street. It was one of the first hotels in New York City to have telephone service. It was also partially made of steel, which made Hannah feel safer, given that many large hotels had burned to the ground in recent years. They would have preferred the new Waldorf-Astoria, but it was not yet completed and would have been too ostentatious for Hannah, whose socialist mind-set did not allow for displays of wealth. Henry did not share that reticence. He believed he was free to choose where he lived, what he wore, and with whom he would be seen. For Henry, socialism was demonstrated through words and actions, and displays of wealth could sometimes be helpful.

Henry noticed that an electric trolley system had replaced the old cable cars, but they took a horse and carriage to the hotel to avoid wrestling their luggage aboard a streetcar. As they rode to the hotel, Henry was shocked by the maze of telephone and electric lines overhead. He was told the city had passed an ordinance that would soon place the wires underground. With so many beautiful buildings, it was a shame to mar the landscape with this hodgepodge of wires.

Sky of wires, New York City, 1892

Their rooms at the Gilsey were small but included large, lovely marble bathrooms. It was a good thing her anarchist friends could not see Hannah in the enormous bathtub. Henry and Hannah both liked staying near the center of town, within walking distance of many of the major theatres. Passing the Union Square Theatre one day, Henry noticed a billboard advertising "Saints and Sinners" starring Countess Helena Modjeska. Henry was secretly thrilled to see the countess's name on the marquee. He knew Helena slightly. She had bought property in Orange County and lived there part of each year. He had been tempted to call her when he lived in Fullerton but never did. Hannah could be insanely jealous.

The small Wilshire family took a carriage around the city. Henry had not been to New York for several years, and it was interesting to see how it had grown. He was disappointed to see that progress on Central Park had stalled. The last time he was there thousands of trees and shrubs had been planted, and he had expected the park to be alive with greenery and color. Instead there were dead trees and sheep foraging on the grass. He had read that Tammany Hall operatives were being accused of using money intended for the park for their own uses.

They saw the newly completed New York World and New York Tribune buildings that Hannah thought decadent and Henry saw as beautiful. The World Building—the first skyscraper to surpass in height the 284-foot spire of Trinity Church—was reportedly 26 stories high, but Henry thought that was an exaggeration.

World Building and New York Tribune Building

They had the carriage take them over the new Brooklyn Bridge that connected Manhattan and Brooklyn over the East River. It was said to be the longest suspension bridge in the world. The ride over the metal and wood paving was thrilling, but Dora was afraid to look down. Henry loved Brooklyn for the trees planted along the busy streets, the red brick row houses, and the attractive small shops.

The highlight of their tour was seeing the Statue of Liberty. They took a boat out to see it along with a hundred other tourists. The sight of the grand lady holding a torch and staring majestically out to sea was an inspiration. The words printed along the base could have been written by a socialist and brought tears to Henry's and Hannah's eyes.

> *"Keep ancient lands, your storied pomp! "Cries she*
> *With silent lips. "Give me your tired, your poor,*
> *Your huddled masses yearning to breathe free,*
> *The wretched refuse of your teeming shore.*
> *Send these, the homeless, tempest-tost to me,*
> *I lift my lamp beside the golden door!"*

A week after their arrival, Henry received a message from Adolphus, an old socialist friend, inviting him to lunch at Café Martin on 26th Street. Adolphus said only that it was an important meeting with some leading socialists. Henry sent a note confirming he would attend. When he arrived at Café Martin the next day, sitting next to Adolphus was Henry George, the single-tax proponent whom Henry had met at the Bohemian Club in San Francisco. Henry knew that George, who had moved to New York a decade before, had run for mayor in 1886, coming in second to a Tammany Hall candidate but besting a young upstate New Yorker named Theodore Roosevelt. George was a favorite of New York's Irish population and had given many lectures in Ireland. Unfortunately the Catholic Church did not share his views on the ownership of property and turned many Catholic voters against George's candidacy.

George stood when Henry approached the table. "Henry Wilshire, as I live and breathe, it is good to see you. How long has it been? Too long I am sure. I heard you had moved to Los Angeles."

They shook hands, and George introduced him to two other men at the table: Lucien Sanial, editor of the *Workmen's Advocate* and one the nation's leading socialist writers, and Daniel De Leon, another socialist leader who was editor of *The People*. The fact that such important political figures wanted to have lunch with him piqued Henry's interest enormously. A waiter took their orders, and after some small talk, Henry asked the question that was foremost in his mind. "Gentlemen, I am sincerely flattered that such important socialists have asked me to lunch. It is indeed an honor, but I am at a loss as to why I am here."

"Let me begin," George replied. "Henry, when you ran for Congress in the Sixth Congressional District in California, you became the first socialist to run for office in the United States. You must know that you caught the attention of the Socialist Labor Party. We also read your editorial in your small weekly newspaper explaining why it is less important to win an election than to get socialist ideas before the public. I could not have written it better myself. As you know, I ran for mayor of New York City and lost. But I won in the sense that I was able to tell the public what I believe. I plan to run again, and, as before, the primary goal will be promoting the socialist agenda."

Henry replied, "Like you, I am deeply committed to the cause. The time is ripe for socialists to stop bickering among themselves and unite to challenge the trusts and greed that threaten to ruin our way of life."

"Henry, it is a pleasure to hear you speak those words," Sanial responded. "I have read your little newspaper, and as a newspaperman myself, I admire your ability to express yourself. We are pleased you have come to New York City. As you already know, this is a hotbed of American socialism, but there are many challenges of which you may not be aware. If you do not mind, I would like to give you a little background on where the party stands today."

Henry replied, "This is fascinating. Please tell me more."

"As of 1886, the Socialist Labor Party had been in existence for nearly a dozen years without making any headway," Sanial continued. "The party's membership consisted predominantly of German immigrants, and some meetings were conducted entirely in German. There was a need to Americanize the movement. We ran Henry George for mayor because he was supported by Irish Americans and was broadly respected as an American who wanted the best for America and for its people. The ideas he put forth in his book *Progress and Poverty* about human dignity and brotherhood appeal to many working people, and his ideas about land taxation are easy for the common man to understand. But we are not the only ones courting the working class. Unionism has become a major force in America, and the American Federation of Labor claims it is the legitimate voice of the workingman. It appeals to the workers' desire for higher wages and better working conditions. The AF of L claims socialism is all talk and will provide few practical benefits for workers."

It was De Leon's turn to speak. "Henry, how much do you know about Samuel Gompers and the American Federation of Labor?"

"I know that he is an extremely powerful man and that he has challenged the Socialist Labor Party on several occasions." Henry said.

"Right you are," De Leon replied. "The Knights of Labor was a weak organization that was based on better working conditions, higher wages, and shorter workdays. Gompers, leading a group of rebels from the International Cigar Makers Union, demonstrated that a union was a model of efficiency and unity. He soon unionized carpenters, typographers, iron molders, tailors—a total of twenty-five groups in less than a year. He is the most successful union organizer in the country and has tried very hard to separate the labor movement from socialism and particularly anarchist ideology. He believes, and is probably correct, that the average American despises extremism in any form. In fact, violence like that of the Haymarket riot a few years ago put socialism and trade unionism in a bad light. The Haymarket riot is what really destroyed the Knights of Labor. As you probably know, the bomb that was thrown in Haymarket Square in 1886 had nothing to do with organized labor but that horrible act caused the Knights of Labor to lose control of their membership as well as any positive public opinion."

George explained: "Socialists were responsible for organizing the Socialist Labor Party of America, which they hoped would attract union members drawn to Marxist principles. Last year Gompers and his AF of L challenged the Socialist Labor Party, also known as the Central Labor Union. Lucian here was sent to Detroit by the Socialist Party to represent them at the joint Labor Party conference and defend the Socialist Labor Party from attack. Gompers told the credentials committee not to seat Lucian as a delegate because that would give other political and economic groups the right to a delegate, thereby causing disunity within the movement. His argument won out, and Lucien was denied a seat at the conference. Lucien will take the debate over socialism versus trade unionism to the International Labor Congress next month in London. At this time, we see no benefit to challenging Gompers directly. We will attempt to have our voice heard in more subtle ways. This is where you come in."

"I am beginning to understand," Henry said. "Please go on."

De Leon took another turn. "Last year the Congress passed the Sherman Antitrust Law aimed at stopping the trusts and the monopolies we all despise. The law makes it a misdemeanor to form any contract or participate in commerce among the states or with foreign nations that is an unreasonable restraint of trade. Enforcement is to be made by district attorneys or by the attorneys general of the states. While we welcome control of the trusts, the law could also be used against us. It could be argued that labor unions and others demonstrating against the system are restraining trade. We do not know if Gompers is going to try to influence public opinion regarding demonstrations, but we have come to the conclusion that we need to run someone for New York attorney general who is an unknown and shares our principles. We want someone articulate who can be seen as a rich man running on behalf of the workingman. Henry, we believe you are just the man we need. Will you run?"

Henry was taken aback. "Gentlemen, I am flattered but am neither a legal resident of this state nor an attorney. I am not qualified for that office."

"The state constitution does not require the attorney general to have a law degree," George explained. "It only says you have to be a citizen of the United States and at least thirty years old. On your birthday next month, you will qualify on both counts."

"You have no reputation in this state," Sanial added. "It is unlikely you will win, but as we have discussed, victory is not the ultimate objective. This election offers a platform to make your views known in the largest city in the nation. The world will recognize you as the level-headed, rational socialist that you are. One of us would run, but we are too well-known and have been labeled—unfairly, I might add—as radicals. Will you do it? Will you run?"

Excited and extremely flattered, Henry thought about it for only a moment. The campaign would delay his trip to London, but the election was just six months away. Hannah could go on ahead, and he would follow after he had lost the election. It was a chance to make his mark before the nation and perhaps the world. It was an opportunity he could not pass up. He agreed to run.

The election was held in November 1891, and Henry lost, receiving fewer than 2,000 votes. His arguments against applying the restraint of trade clause of the Sherman Antitrust Law to unions were heard in Washington, D.C., and the Supreme Court. Although his arguments did not succeed, the name Henry Gaylord Wilshire began to be recognized. The Millionaire Socialist had established himself as a prominent socialist. He was also recognized as a man of peace and non-violence. His wife, Hannah, was not helpful in his attempt to downplay any tie to anarchy or communism.

While in New York, Hannah had met the famous anarchist Emma Goldman, who was a great influence on her. Emma had arrived in the United States in 1885 from what is now Lithuania. She came from a conservative Jewish family; her father had once thrown her French book into the fireplace and told her, "All a Jewish girl needs to know is how to prepare gefilte fish, cut noodles fine, and give the man plenty of chicken." Emma, of course, had a mind of her own and ignored the ridiculous maxim.

Emma related to the Sonya character in Dostoyevsky's "Crime and Punishment." Sonya sacrificed nearly everything for her friend Raskolnikov. Emma bought a pistol for her lover, Alexander Berkman. In 1892, Berkman would use the pistol in an unsuccessful attempt to kill a factory manager whom he considered an enemy of the people. Typical of a number of anarchists of the time, Emma would have died for the sake of "the people." These ideologues no longer believed in a benign and omnipotent God, instead putting their faith in a new "divinity" – the people. Free living and free loving, Goldman had worked in New York sweatshops and had a peculiar power to sway audiences. She was painfully aware of the impoverished women in the tenement houses. She saw starvation, prostitution, alcoholism, and terrible poverty. New York City, the supposed city of opportunity, was a trash heap for hundreds of thousands of people. When speaking to crowds, Goldman often urged them to take up arms against the evil capitalists. In the years after the assassination attempt, she was arrested and spent several months in prison. She condemned communists who were not willing to pay the price of their convictions.

Hannah was inspired by the abstract, religious nature of the ideology. For her, the term "the people" inspired all the fervor and passion that a priest or nun felt for the name "Jesus Christ." When Hannah learned that Emma might be deported she wept. That a brave and honorable woman should be so mistreated for her beliefs was a crime. Hannah also read many of the writings of Prince Kropotkin—"the Anarchist Prince" who had also been jailed in Russia for his activism—and learned of his predictions that the people would someday throw off the bonds of serfdom.

Hannah loved and admired Henry, but she did not respect his views about democratic capitalism. She found his idea that capitalism was inherently good to be naïve. Capitalism is based on greed and selfishness and as such could not be good. Only when mankind accepted that property should be shared and distributed equally according to need would there be peace in the world. She also did not believe that democracy was always the best political system. Sometimes a dictatorship is necessary because people do not always act in their own best interest. Like children, they need a benevolent guardian to guide them. She also agreed with the anarchists that violence should sometimes be used to accomplish what could not be achieved through peaceful means. As one anarchist put it, "Bullets are better than votes sometimes."

She also did not agree with her husband's editorial that said, "There is only one day in the year when the American people have any power, and that is on Election Day." Hannah believed that violence instead of votes was sometimes necessary to force real reforms.

While Henry was running for attorney general, Hannah went on to London and stayed for a time with her family in Wales. She also met Prince Kropotkin. The prince was on his way to Russia but had a beautiful home in Hampstead Heath near London. He offered it to Hannah to use until she and Henry found their own place, and Hannah gladly accepted. Hampstead Heath was a lovely park area with small lakes, walking paths, horse trails, gardens, and vast lawns. It was one of the most beautiful neighborhoods in suburban London. Hannah and Dora enjoyed living there a great deal until Henry arrived from New York.

Henry got to London the week before Christmas in 1891. He traveled by a large coach from the dock to Piccadilly Circus, where Hannah was to meet him. Like New York, London was an exhilarating city that made him feel alive. Piccadilly Square was as picturesque as ever with its large fountain and statue of Eros standing at the crossroads of Regent Street with Piccadilly. Henry could not help but compare the streets of London with those of New York, San Francisco, and Los Angeles. The biggest difference was the color of the buildings: London's were stained with hundreds of years of coal smoke. The Thames was dirty, and vagrants were everywhere. It appeared to be a city in decline. Piccadilly Circus, however, looked like the large street he envisioned for Long Beach and Fullerton. Perhaps he would get another chance to design a boulevard to his liking.

Piccadilly Square – London– around 1895

Hannah met Henry with a fervent embrace and a smile on her face. She was obviously glad to see him. He had so many things on his mind that his embrace was slightly indifferent. But he was pleased that Prince Kropotkin had let them use his home in

Hampstead Heath until they could find a place of their own. Henry knew Hampstead and its large park, lakes, and riding trails. It would be a good place to think.

He had the names and letters of introduction to several young socialists in London. His recent campaign for state attorney general had filled his mind with visions of things to come. He had some serious reading to do about the Fabian Society, a group advocating a new brand of thought that was sweeping London. He knew he would be asked for his opinion.

Henry contacted several of the people suggested by Henry George and Lucien Sanial. At the top of the list was the Countess of Warwick, a new recruit to the socialist cause. She was the wife of Francis Greville, or Lord Brooke, the eldest son of George Greville, the fourth Earl of Warwick. The Warwicks owned the landmark Warwick Castle. The countess was also known as Daisy and was most often referred to by that name in the press. Daisy had a lover or two who were more prominent than her husband, an acceptable practice in the Victorian era, given that husbands often benefited politically or socially from such arrangements. The countess was the mistress of several powerful men, most notably Edward VII. She liked to brag about her lovers, which earned her the nickname "The Babbling Brooke."

Journalist Robert Blanchard wrote a critique of Warwick's lifestyle, causing her to turn to socialism. She found she had real empathy for the poor, elderly, and children, and began a number of charities and projects to help those in need. She often threw dinner parties for leading socialists at her home in

London. Henry and Hannah were invited not three months after they arrived in London. They were pleased to accept the invitation.

*The Countess of Warwick (Daisy Greville) truly
glamorous and a hostess for many socialist causes*

When they arrived at Warwick Manor, as the house was called, they were impressed by the great luxury. Gorgeous paintings hung on the walls, and sumptuous carpets were spread across shining wooden floors. The carpets—so exquisite one hesitated to walk on them—must have been imported from some far-off, exotic locale. Large chandeliers hung from the ceiling in several rooms, and busts and statues stood as sentinels lining the stairways. There were high, coffered ceilings with carved cornices overhead. Two large marble pillars stood on either side of the large doorway that led into the parlor. A mix of wood smoke and cooked beef filled the air, and a large fire was blazing in the fireplace. A well-dressed butler ushered them into a large parlor. There were several people sitting or standing with glasses of wine or punch in their hands.

Countess Warwick stood and approached Henry and Hannah. She was a tall, attractive woman with bright blue eyes and lovely hair that must have taken hours to create. She immediately took Hannah's arm and Henry's hand and said, "Welcome to my home. We were so pleased when we heard you were coming to London. I have heard such good things about both of you. Prince Kropotkin has told me, Hannah, about you being one his favorite students, and Henry George tells us that you, Henry, have a great future in the party. Welcome, comrades. London and the party need you here."

Hannah said, "The prince told me about you as well. It is a privilege to meet a woman as famous as you are who has finally seen the light."

Henry thought Hannah's remark was a little patronizing and decided to change the subject. "Countess, you are known for your dinner parties and your interesting guests. I hope we are up to the challenge. Is that the playwright George Bernard Shaw over there? I am a great admirer."

"He will be so pleased to hear that. He can't resist a devotee of his work. You should tell him yourself. Come, I will introduce you."

George Bernard Shaw – playwright, critic and author

They crossed the room, and Shaw was engaged in what seemed like an argument with a dark-haired man wearing a monocle. "George, I have a new admirer for your club," the countess interrupted. "I would like you to meet Henry Gaylord Wilshire, the first socialist to run for Congress in the United States, and his wife, Hannah, a good friend of Prince Kropotkin."

Shaw was thin with a nicely trimmed beard and an impish smile that suggested he loved to tease. "Ah, new blood for the socialist cause. Tell me, are Americans still dumping tea into the harbor, or have they come to their senses about not wasting good tea?"

"We are more concerned about dumping capitalists into the sea. Preferably with an anchor around their necks," Hannah replied.

"Now, now, dear, Mr. Shaw will think we are violent people. I have read some of your articles in the Fabian Weekly, and I agree with some of your thinking about the gradual reform of government and capitalism. But I think some of your ideas about government ownership of land would not go over in the States."

Shaw said sarcastically, "It's so good of you to consider that those of us on this side of the Atlantic might have a good idea or two."

The man with the monocle said, "America is new to socialism. I realize you are still being pragmatic in your attempts at reform, but I believe Fabian socialism has a future in the States."

"May I introduce Mr. Sidney Webb, the new founder of the London School of Economics and a newlywed," the countess said.

A woman no older than twenty approached and said, "May I add that I am the co-founder of the London School of Economics, and Sidney is my husband."

Sydney and Beatrice Webb – Founders of the London School of Economics

"Ah, yes, we mustn't forget the young bride in our midst. May I present Beatrice Potter, also known as Mrs. Sidney Webb? Do not let her youthful appearance fool you. Most of us think she is brilliant and knows more about economic theory than people three times her age."

"I do hope that is not a dig about her new husband," Sidney joked.

Hannah said, "It is wonderful to find a country that recognizes that women have an intelligent voice to contribute to society. Do you know Emma Goldman, Mrs. Potter?"

"Just call me Beatrice. I dislike formality. Yes, I have heard of Mrs. Goldman. She is an anarchist who was jailed for a time for inciting a mob to violence, and she also is said to have purchased a weapon that was used in an assassination attempt."

"She is a proud anarchist who recognizes that a woman must sometimes provide the weapons for revolution," Hannah said, bristling. "The people demand much of the party's workers. No price is too high if true revolution is to take place."

Countess Warwick saw tension growing on the faces of the small group. "Henry and Hannah, let me introduce you to some of the other guests." She took Hannah's arm and whisked her and Henry across the room to a short young man seated next to a tall, attractive woman. "Henry and Hannah, I would like you to meet Mr. H.G. Wells, the writer and teacher, and Miss Elinor Glyn, the novelist and one of my closest friends."

Henry smiled and said, "Miss Glyn, I have read one of your books. Sexy stuff, if I may say so."

Library of Congress
Elinor Glyn – novelist and screenwriter

Elinor replied, "I am so glad if I aroused you in some way, Henry. Have you read any of my books, Hannah?'

"I try not to read books that will in any way distract me from socialist ideals. Is your book about socialism? That is hardly sexy."

"Elinor's books do not concern socialism unless you include the free love element of the party," Wells said. "Glad to meet you both. Are you going to live in London? "

"We plan to stay for some time," Henry said. "What is your occupation, Mr. Wells?"

H. G. Wells – author and historian

"I am a student of history. I also fancy myself a writer. I teach at a secondary school to earn my keep. I overheard you mention your interest in the Fabian Society. I flirted with joining, but their ideas are not creative enough for my tastes. I prefer looking at the world as a whole. I also like to write fiction that deals with futurism. Do you like futuristic writing, Hannah?"

"Not unless it deals with the future of stomping capitalist warmongers beneath the heels of the socialist movement," Hannah replied.

"I must say, I prefer my bedroom scenes to your class wars. Much more fun," Elinor joked to laughter from the men.

Henry knew he was going to like London. He had just met six fascinating people and wanted to hear more about their views and interests. He was a little embarrassed by Hannah's comments, which were neither interesting nor witty. He found her thinking to be simple and her delivery bombastic. Henry noticed how young all those in attendance were.

A servant entered the room and whispered something to the countess. "Ladies and gentlemen, I am pleased to announce that dinner is ready and will be served in the next room," she said.

The dining room had crystal chandeliers overhead, and large candlesticks served as centerpieces on the table. Each place setting had several crystal wine glasses, two china dinner plates, and a small salad plate stacked on top. The seating arrangements were formal, and Henry saw there were place cards. He was seated next to Countess Warwick and Hannah next to George Bernard Shaw. He knew that could be trouble.

The servants brought in tureens of hot soup and began serving.

Shaw turned to Hannah and said, "Tell me, my dear, have you shot any capitalists lately?"

Hannah looked startled.

"Probably not," the countess interjected, "but perhaps she should shoot a few playwrights I know."

There was laughter from the group.

"Seriously, Hannah, does Kropotkin believe that by assassinating leaders of government you can achieve socialist ends? Certainly he must understand that violence only provokes them," Wells said.

"The prince believes in giving power to the people. Sometimes power only comes from the end of a gun," Hannah replied.

"But guns can be used both ways, can't they?" Beatrice asked. "Kings and queens have killed hundreds if not thousands of innocent people caught in the middle of a class conflict. Surely there are better ways to achieve our ends than through violence?"

"There are always casualties in a struggle for freedom," Henry said.

Sidney Webb smiled. "My wife's definition of 'the people' is romantic. I, for one, am not sure the people have any interest in government and political struggles. They are more interested in feeding their families—practical things rather than abstract notions."

"There comes a time, however, when practicality is supplanted by a refusal of those with money and power to provide the opportunity for the people to earn a fair wage and an adequate standard of living," the countess said. "The people may learn that abstractions like liberty, fairness, and equal opportunity are more than just words," she continued, as tears formed in the corners of her eyes.

Changing the subject, Shaw complimented the countess on the meal. "The soup is delicious. I must have this recipe. Did you make this, countess?"

"I am known more for my stews than my soups. That is why I give these lovely dinner parties. I like to create new mixtures."

Henry said, "Was I invited as an onion or as a potato? I must say I would rather be an onion."

"I would not worry about being an onion," Shaw said. "There is too much spice in Daisy's stews these days. She needs a potato or two to take the edge off. Potatoes stay with you long after onions have soiled your breath and constipated your will."

"Enough talk about stews and onions, Shaw," the countess said. "I want to know what the Fabians are going to do about the coming revolution in Russia. Shaw, you and Sidney are part of their inner circle. How will this group of timid reformers deal with a radical movement?"

"The Fabian Society is more interested in an eight-hour day and better working conditions for Britons than in the constant struggle between the proletariat and the nobles in Moscow," he said. "What happens after we nationalize the land is more important to me than providing red flags for demonstrators in Saint Petersburg."

Shaw added, "May I remind the dinner party that the Fabian Society is named after 'the delayer,' Quintus Fabius Maximus? As much as I hate to agree with a sociologist, Beatrice's point is well-taken. Sometimes reform—a delaying action if you please—must come gradually rather than through violence. I understand, Sidney, that you and Beatrice have written a new study of industrial Great Britain that argues for cooperative ownership of capital as well as land. Is that correct?"

Beatrice frowned. "My goodness, Shaw, you are well-informed. We have not finished our study yet. You must have spies everywhere."

"Never underestimate a playwright's imagination, my dear. What they lack in facts they make up as fiction," her husband said. "You are correct, my dear friend, our system of cooperative ownership would be accomplished through what we called 'collective bargaining,' a process whereby capital and labor negotiate to satisfy the needs of both groups without strikes and certainly without armed conflict."

"No such agreement will ever last for long," Hannah said. "Capitalists will only lull you to sleep with their supposed agreements and stab the workingman in the back when he least expects it."

"What has made such a lovely woman so bitter?" Wells asked. "Are not capitalists made of the same flesh and blood as the rest of us, and do they not need to compromise in order to achieve peace? I am a zoologist by training, and one thing I learned about animals is that every species can live peacefully together if they have a common need. Capital and labor need each other. One cannot exist without the other. My complaint with the Fabians is that they lack imagination. They must look to the entire world, not just England, for the solutions to the globe's economic ills."

Daisy laughed and said, "You are all ruining my lovely dinner with your talk of violence and socialist causes. Doesn't anyone have some gossip to tell? Who is sleeping with whom, and which leaders are stealing from the public coffers?"

Beatrice responded, "This is a marvelous segue to ask Glyn about sexual interests and appetites. Do your erotic novels have an equal market between men and women? Are women just as interested in what makes a good lover as men are? Do married people or lovers read your books to each other?"

Elinor answered, "I have no way of knowing the answer to those questions. When I write my books I always assume that women and men have an equal interest in sexual conquests and techniques. My books are intended to entertain, not instruct. You are correct when you insinuate they are also meant to arouse an interest in sex. Sex, like economics, makes strange bedfellows—although sex brings passion and economics brings boredom. In answer to your question about who buys more erotic books, I don't really know. Bookshops do not record who buys my books. I just hope that both sexes continue to enjoy a tantalizing and arousing tale and continue to turn loose with the money to satisfy their sexual interests."

Beatrice added, "I would not agree that economics is boring, but I can see where sex could be depending on those who put in the data."

Everyone laughed once again.

Shaw said, "Is there no data on sexual practice? How disappointing. Perhaps my next play will deal with those kinds of sexual issues. What a grand idea. If I make it into a play I shall give you credit Elinor."

"If it is anything like your last play, you need a little sex to keep the audience from nodding off," the countess teased.

Everyone howled at that.

The dinner and conversation continued for another two hours. When he got home, Henry was so excited by the quality of the conversation and the repartee that he could not sleep. What a wonderful dinner and what fascinating people. Hannah said she was bored with the group and found the conversation silly. Henry told her he thought the conversation was witty and he had learned a great deal from the discussion. Henry thought to himself how Hannah could be such a bore.

Henry, Hannah, and Dora lived in Kropotkin's house for only a short time before they found a small house to rent in central London. Henry attended some meetings of the Fabian Society and found that, while their notion that capitalism could be saved through reforms alone had merit, their views on land ownership did not. Property was the key to power in America, and nationalizing the railroads, steel mills, and coal mines could be a good thing for the country. Henry believed companies like United States Steel, Standard Oil of Ohio, and the Union Pacific Railroad should be owned by the government. The Fabians advocated control of many large corporations as well. Railroads, coal mines, steel mills might not be owned by the government, but taxation would keep them under some government regulation. They also believed in the nationalization of land and borrowed heavily from the ideas of Henry George.

Hannah, of course, would simply shoot the corporate owners and be done with it. Her answers to complex economic problems often boiled down to simplistic answers. Sometimes he wondered how he could have married such a violent woman. Perhaps her upbringing was why she saw violence as an acceptable way to solve problems. He never found out.

The Socialist Party of Great Britain decided it was time to run a candidate for Parliament who could take their views to the public. They knew they could not defeat the Fabian candidates or the Conservative Party with its Marquess of Salisbury. Henry had become a British citizen in 1893 and had dual citizenship. The British Socialist Party asked him to run for Parliament in 1894. He agreed.

About the time Henry decided to run for Parliament, Hannah decided to return to Wales. They had been bickering for more than a year, and it was obvious their marriage was failing. Their political differences were part of the problem, as was Hannah's fiery temper. They separated, and Henry took a small apartment in London.

It became obvious to him that he needed to return to America and Los Angeles. Henry had been receiving funds from his walnut and almond orchards in Orange County and the investments his brother William had made for him in San Francisco. He decided he needed to get back to business and do something with that thirty-five-acre parcel he had purchased a decade ago. He left for America in 1894 and filed for divorce in Los Angeles. Hannah did not contest the divorce as long as she received part of the orchards. Henry agreed, and the divorce was granted in 1895.

"I am glad to get rid of the fiery piece of Welsh rarebit," he wrote to a friend. Henry never learned how many votes he received in his run for Parliament.

Security Pacific National Bank Collection/ Los Angeles Public Library
Plans for Wilshire Blvd. in 1900

CHAPTER 5
The Boulevard to the Sea

When Henry returned to Los Angeles, he found much had changed in the six years he was gone. The railroad station, now at Sixth and Main streets, was the nexus of the Los Angeles Yellow Street Car Line and the large railroads. The city's population had exploded to create a teeming city of roughly 100,000 compared to the mere 11,000 residents in 1885, when Henry had purchased his 35-acre barley field. Many people were coming west for health reasons or for retirement, while others came to work in the citrus orchards, the movie industry or the growing manufacturing sector.

As a horse-drawn cab took him to his hotel, Henry noticed new electric streetlights, paved streets, and electric poles along each street. Apparently the city was too poor to put the electric lines underground as Henry had seen in New York City. Handsome new buildings were going up everywhere. Bunker Hill was still popular with the rich and famous, but now apartment houses and inexpensive hotels lined Main, Spring, and Los Angeles streets along with theaters, banks, and retail stores. In just a decade, Los Angeles had become a major city. There were many more automobiles parked at curbs. Henry believed that automobiles would play a major role in Los Angeles due to how spread out the city had and would become.

Security Pacific National Bank Collection/Los Angeles Public Library
**Fashion, automobiles, sidewalks, and well dressed women begin to
demonstrate how Los Angeles had continued to modernize**

Los Angeles had changed and Henry knew he had changed
as well. He had learned some things about himself. He knew his
socialist calling was more than a passing interest. He believed
he was meant to become a national leader of the socialist cause.
Henry had met key leaders of the movement in both the United
States and Britain, and had earned their respect and even their
admiration. His own political philosophy was clearer, and he
felt more strongly than ever that reforms could save American
capitalism. Fabian socialism had influenced his ideas about the

need for gradual reform, and his aversion to Hannah's radicalism had helped him become more moderate in his thinking. He had never advocated violence, but now he was certain the written word was the most powerful weapon one could use against the trusts.

He also knew it was important that he make a great deal of money—to advance socialism's causes as well as his own. Henry liked the finer things and always had. Tailored clothes, a nice home, fine wine and good food were important to him. He also liked mingling with the rich and famous. Wealth often meant power and intelligence, and he believed he belonged in that sphere of influence.

One of the first things Henry did was visit his property. It was still marshy, full of weeds, and smelled like oil. The neighboring Sunset Park remained full of brown weeds and dead trees. In contrast, Westlake Park on the eastern edge of the property was improving nicely. There were flower beds and riding trails that led to a lovely small lake. Small sailboats and rowboats were available for hire. Lovers strolled hand-in-hand along the walking paths. His property was bounded by Sixth Street to the north and Seventh Street to the south. Both went directly to the downtown area, but they were still unpaved and pretty primitive.

Henry hired a surveyor to draw the property's boundaries and began to think about clearing and developing the land. He had always loved street planning and enthusiastically set about designing his boulevard. He knew developing the land would take money so he contacted his brother William in San Francisco. William, who was co-owner of the property, had banker friends in the California Club who might be interested in their plan.

It took three months to clear the land. William had sent sufficient funds to get started, and Henry used some of his inheritance. Henry decided the best approach was to develop a small portion of the acreage into a short street as a sample of what was to come. The sketch showed a paved 2,000-yard street with curbs, cement sidewalks, streetlights, and palm trees. He imagined unique mansions set back a good distance from the new boulevard and smaller but beautiful homes on the side streets. The sketch showed Westlake Park in the background and the cityscape on the horizon. It would be a model street for the city of Los Angeles. In Henry's mind, their thirty-five acres would become in one of the city's best neighborhoods. It was near the downtown area, yet set apart, and no trucks, trolley cars or large conveyances would be allowed. Henry saw the development as a first step in creating a major development that would extend all the way to Santa Monica and other developed beach cities.

The rather primitive El Camino Viejo was still used as a path to the sea by wagons and horse carts filled with coal, sand, manure, and other goods from the ports in Redondo and Santa Monica. A streetcar line was used primarily by beach- and party-goers. There was clearly a need for a large road to carry freight.

Other wealthy men also saw the need to connect downtown Los Angeles with the sea. John P. Jones, a wealthy gold-mine owner and a former United States senator from Nevada, had purchased a three-quarter interest in Colonel Robert S. Baker's ranch in Santa Monica and had laid out a well-designed city near the ocean. He built a hotel called The Miramar that was so large its turrets were visible from downtown Los Angeles on a clear day. Jones also built a small railroad called the Los Angeles and Independence Railroad that traveled on a narrow gauge line between Santa Monica and Los Angeles. The line linked Redondo and other small ports with Santa Monica. Another developer, Abbott Kinney, was making plans of his own for a beach city called Venice that would have canals and gondolas like its famous Italian namesake.

Miramar Hotel in Santa Monica – Luxury Near the Ocean

Financial hardship forced Jones to sell his small railroad to Collis P. Huntington, who was planning a mile-long wharf off the shore of Santa Monica. A war was going on between Collis P. and Phineas Banning as to whether the official Port of Los Angeles would be located in Santa Monica or San Pedro. Banning and John G. Downey had already built a 21-mile railway called the Los Angeles and San Pedro Railroad between their San Pedro Harbor and the city. Henry could see it was going to be a major fight between the Banning and Huntington as to where the Port of Los Angeles would be located. Unfortunately Banning died before he saw the end of the battle.

Huntington's Long Wharf near Santa Monica

Unfortunately for Huntington, Banning and Downey had more friends on the city council and more friends in Washington than he did and their plan for San Pedro and Wilmington became the official harbor of Los Angeles. Huntington died in 1900 having lost his battle for his Long Wharf.

Phineas Banning

Los Angeles was growing rapidly, and Henry knew he had to move fast if he were going to be the first to develop a route to the ocean. He filed subdivision papers on December 21, 1895, which allowed him to develop the land. The subdivision butted into the middle of Westlake Park and was now clearly part of the city development map. Developing the land was the first step, and he accomplished it in six months.

The time was right for a path to the sea. The downtown area was well-developed, and rich businessmen and industrialists were building large homes across the river in Boyle Heights.

Bunker Hill remained home to the well-to-do, and wealthy newcomers were arriving every day. Los Angeles boasted a new City Hall, a cathedral, a university, 78 miles of paved streets, and an architectural jewel called the Bradbury Building. A small railroad line was extended to the new town of Pasadena about ten miles east of the city.

The rest of the nation was in a depression, but Los Angeles was booming. Edward Doheny had struck oil close to the downtown. Wells were sprouting up everywhere on the outskirts, and the City Council was hard-pressed to keep oil wells from overwhelming the landscape. The council fought to keep the city green and built Sixth Street Park in the center of the downtown. A large land developer named Griffith J. Griffith advanced their cause in December 1896 by donating 3,000 acres for a park. A prohibitionist couple had started a lovely area called Hollywood in the northwestern part of the city. And John Wolfskill, a former forty-niner who had made a fortune with his Santa Monica Land and Water Company, had formed a subdivision called Sunset. Wolfskill was practically giving away small parcels of agricultural land to friends. A section of the former Rancho Rodeo de las Aguas was being subdivided, including one large section called Beverly Hills. Wolfskill was also selling lots on parcels he owned nearer downtown Los Angeles. He planted large palm trees along Central Avenue to make the avenue seem something it wasn't, since palm trees are not native to California.

There was so much development going on it was difficult for Henry and William to keep track of the expansion. Along the

Southern Pacific Railroad line, small towns were sprouting up all the way to San Bernardino with names like Arcadia, El Monte, San Dimas, Sierra Madre, Monrovia, Pomona, Claremont, Ontario, Rancho Cucamonga, and Riverside. Citrus and cattle ranches dotted the new areas. Water battles occurred in some areas like Azusa, Gladstone, and Glendora. It was a time of significant and long-lasting change in Southern California and particularly Los Angeles. The time for the Boulevard to the Sea was now. It could not wait.

Henry had learned a great deal about land development from the Amerige brothers in Fullerton—namely that you sometimes benefited from giving something away. He decided to give his short boulevard to the city if the council would let him develop the adjacent properties. He would impose some conditions: no heavy freight or streetcar tracks. But he would pave the street and put in streetlights, sidewalks and trees at his own expense. It would be a good deal for the city. How could the council refuse?

Henry contacted his new friend John Haynes. The physician, a socialist whom John had met at the California Club, had made a small fortune in recent years as a real estate speculator. A leading citizen, he was a Democrat with friends in the Republican Party. Haynes liked Henry's plan and agreed to use his influence to get Henry before the Los Angeles City Council.

*John R. Haynes- physician, real estate developer and philanthropist.
Responsible for the initiative and referendum process in California.*

Henry started to rebuild his connections with key Angelenos. He reinstated his membership in the California Club and attended many of its social functions. He also joined a new golf club that had developed a nine-hole course not far from his parcel. A golf course could be a great friend to a land developer. Homebuyers would appreciate the park-like setting, and a new course was bound to attract many city fathers and leading businessmen.

Haynes was able to get Henry a half-hour to present his plan at the City Council's next meeting. Henry was thrilled. He hired an artist to draw a professional sketch of his plan that, when completed, could easily have been mistaken for a beautiful landscape painting.

The City Council met in the new City Hall on Spring Street. It overlooked St. Vibiana's Cathedral and was close to the old heart of Los Angeles. The Pico House and Olvera Street were across the street. City Hall was a wooden, four-story building with bay windows overlooking the street.

1889 Los Angeles city hall between Second and Third Street

Henry walked into the council meeting on time and full of enthusiasm. Sixteen well-dressed men were seated around a long table. The room smelled like fresh furniture wax. There was light streaming through the windows, and the curtains fluttered in the breeze coming through the open windows. Haynes went ahead of Henry and began shaking hands with the men. It was obvious he knew them all.

The head of the City Council was John Tufts, a lawyer. Seated at the table were the mayor, Thomas Rowan, and the former mayor, Henry Hazard. The other thirteen councilmen were doctors, lawyers, and industrialists except for the newspaperman Col. Harrison Gray Otis. He was a powerful-looking man with a face you would not forget.

Calling the meeting to order, Tufts formally introduced Haynes, who in turn introduced Henry.

"Gentlemen, I would like you to meet my good friend Henry Gaylord Wilshire. Many of you know Henry from his contributions to the cities of Long Beach and Fullerton. He is a man of great genius in my estimation. He has been living in Britain the past few years, and I welcome him back to Los Angeles. We need his insight and imagination. He has brought a proposal and some beautiful drawings that he would like to share with the council. May I introduce Henry Gaylord Wilshire."

Henry stood and smiled at the prominent men before him. He knew it was important to appear humble. "Mayor and gentlemen of the council, it is indeed a pleasure to be here today, and I appreciate the opportunity to come before you. I know your time is valuable, and I will try to get right to the point. But before I begin, I would like to say I have been abroad for the past few years, and I would like to congratulate you on the wonderful progress you have made on the city's development. I am also a little disappointed that you made such great progress without my help."

"Rest assured, it was difficult without you," Otis said. He paused, then asked sarcastically, "What was your name again?"

The other councilmen chuckled.

Henry ignored the barb and continued. "I know you are interested in seeing to it that the city expands to the west. The railroads have built a line to the sea. I want to build a boulevard to the sea. The beauty of my plan is that it will cost the city nothing."

"So somebody wants to give us something for nothing," one councilman responded. "It sounds like the old Escrow Indians are alive and well. Be careful, gentlemen, and watch your wallets."

Some of the councilmen laughed. Henry did not.

"Gentlemen, I am an honest man, I assure you. Some of you know how I helped develop the streets of Long Beach and Fullerton. There is even a park in Fullerton with my name on it. While I am civic-minded, this is a business proposition. I would like you to see an artist's sketch that illustrates my plans."

Henry had asked the artist to enlarge the drawing and mount it on a four-by-eight-foot board. Henry placed the sketch on two easels at one end of the long table where the members were seated.

"Gentlemen, what you see before you is a boulevard that will connect downtown Los Angeles to the sea. My brother and I own the property this sketch portrays. The land is cleared but not yet developed. You will notice that the boulevard is quite wide, capable of permitting three carriages or automobiles to travel side-by-side in each direction. I realize there are few automobiles in our city to date, but the automobile will some-day replace the horse and even the railroad as a means of transportation. I believe it important to plan for the future. If you look closely, you will see curbs and asphalt paving, con-crete sidewalks and grass parkways. There will be flower beds at the end of each block. There are electric streetlights, and the power lines are underground, as in New York City. Palm trees will be planted along the major street, and shade trees will line the four side streets, yet to be named. You will notice beautiful homes set back from the street both on the major boulevard and on the side streets. The minimum lot size will be half an acre. Our parcel of land is one mile from downtown and fifteen miles from the ocean. A large artesian well on the property will supply the water."

"You will also notice the land butts up against your beautiful Westlake Park on one end and the undeveloped Sunset Park on the other. We realize that, thanks to Mrs. Clara Shatto's generosity, Sunset Park now belongs to the city. We would be happy to assist with park improvements. Our land also rests between Sixth and Seventh streets. We would suggest running streetcar lines in different directions on the two streets to provide transportation to outlying residents in the western parts of the city, as has been done for Boyle Heights and the areas east of the river. I understand there is also a plan to extend a railcar line to the new city of Pasadena."

"Members of the council, my plan is simple and straightforward. I am proposing to give you the major boulevard shown in the sketch free of charge. You may name it what you will. The boulevard will belong to the city. My condition is that you permit me to develop and sell the residential lots that will be developed on either side of the boulevard and side streets. The benefits to me are obvious, while the city's advantage is that it receives the beginning of a path to the sea. What's more you will receive tax revenue from a first-class housing development.

My only restrictions are that no rail lines along the boulevard or cross streets be permitted and that the city prohibit all heavy vehicles from the roads."

Tufts was the first to speak. "Mr. Wilshire, your plan has a lot going for it. I for one appreciate your honesty and straightforwardness regarding the benefits to both you and the city. The idea of a thoroughfare to the sea is not new, but your plan is attractive. The fact that your parcel borders Westlake Park appeals to me. A street that begins at our lovely park and travels all the way to Santa Monica has real merit. I realize your plan does not go beyond your small parcel, but it is obvious to me that other developers would use your plan as a model for their own developments. This is a concept many of us have pondered, but you are the first to come up with a concrete plan."

Another councilman said, "I, too, think this plan is something we should seriously consider. Should we approve the proposal, I see no reason not to name the thoroughfare Wilshire Boulevard to acknowledge your foresight and generosity. We have precedence have we not, Griffith? Didn't I hear that you were thinking about contributing some of your acreage north of the city for a park if we name it after you?"

"I trust you are joking," Griffith replied. "That property is worth a fortune. The only way I would give it away is if I had no buyers and I needed the money. So far my pockets are not empty, so please do not assume I am headed to the poorhouse just yet."

Snyder said, "Come on, Griffith, you are richer than Rockefeller. The city is thinking of asking you for a loan."

More laughter.

Tufts regained control of the meeting. "Gentlemen, we have a long agenda today. I think we should carefully consider Mr. Wilshire's proposal and get back to him as quickly we can. May we ask you to leave the drawings? We will need to consult with the city engineer and others. We will respond by the end of the month."

"Gentlemen, I would be happy to leave our working drawings. Take all the time you need, but remember that barley planting season is only two months away, and if you do not approve the plan, we need time to get our crop into the ground."

"Sounds like blackmail to me," Mayor Rowan joked, "but as a former farmer, I think you will have plenty of time as long as the rains don't come."

Henry stood and shook hands all around. He and Haynes left the meeting together.

Haynes told Henry that his presentation was excellent—short and to the point. He was sure the city would accept the proposal. Why would they turn it down? The council had nothing to lose and a lot to gain. In particular, they could take credit for the development. Henry did not care who got the credit as long as he could sell the property on either side of the boulevard.

The Los Angeles City Council approved his plan on May 6, 1896. Henry submitted a plot plan to the city engineer. Crossing Wilshire Boulevard were streets he called Park View, Carondelet, Coronado, and Rampart. He received a loan from Security

Trust and Savings Bank. The president of the bank was Joseph A. Sartori, a fellow member of the California Club. The sidewalks and curbs went in first, then the streets were paved and the trees planted. The water lines were completed shortly after the streets went in. Word spread, and Henry began fielding inquiries from potential buyers.

Col. Otis purchased one of the first properties—a large corner lot at Wilshire Boulevard and Park View. It was a prime location with a view of the Hollywood Hills north of the city. Henry saw the plans for the Otis home, called the Bivouac, nearly as soon as they were completed. It was to be a very large Spanish-Moorish mansion, with Ionic columns in front, a red tile roof, and three fireplaces. It would be set back from the street with a double driveway in front and a covered carriage entry on the side. It was large but not ostentatious. Henry was pleased such a lovely home would be one of the first in his development, and he expected it to serve as a model for other houses.

Home of Colonel Harrison Gray Otis called the Bivouac

Henry Gaylord Wilshire had a strange relationship with Harrison Gray Otis. Otis was a large aggressive man with a walrus mustache, a goatee, and a severe demeanor. One author said he resembled Buffalo Bill and General Custer rolled into one. Otis was politically ambitious but never ran for office. He preferred to be the power behind the throne. He was a lifelong Republican and hated Democrats. He called them "hags, harlots, and pollutants." Members of organized labor were "skunks, pinheads, gas-pipe ruffians, rowdies, anarchists, and deadbeats." When the Spanish-American War broke out in 1898, Otis volunteered for service though he was in his early 60s. Because he had previously served under William McKinley, he was given the rank of brigadier general. He was a bully and many people were afraid of him. Henry was not. He considered Otis to be an enemy of the socialist cause but a man to be respected for the power that emanated from his printing press. Otis considered Henry to be a harmless pest. He found his dressing in a tuxedo to give speeches in Sixth Street Park humorous, and Otis' Los Angeles Times sometimes covered Wilshire's antics. It helped that Haynes was Otis' personal physician.

Otis was no fan of Henry Gaylord Wilshire but still purchased one of his first lots on Wilshire Boulevard

Otis was one of the few established Angelenos to purchase a lot from the Wilshires. Most buyers were newcomers with new money and a few entrepreneurs who had made it big in the real estate, light industry or citrus industry. As Henry had hoped, owning a home on or near Wilshire Boulevard was becoming a status symbol. Edwin Tobias Earl, one of the originators of the refrigerated railroad car and owner of the defunct Los Angeles Express, bought a lot next to Otis and built a brick home nearly as large but not as beautiful as the Bivouac. Earl started a new newspaper, the Los Angeles Tribune, which was as liberal as the Times was conservative. Earl and Otis were friendly rivals and frequent guests in each other's new homes. As houses went up, their different architectural styles gave the neighborhood a rather eclectic appearance. Some were built in the new Queen Anne and Eastlake styles with corner towers, splendid verandas, second- and third-floor balconies, and here and there a prideful bit of stained glass. They had diagonal stripes of siding, whorls of round-ended shingles, parti-colored roofing, and English chimneys. They were often painted a tasteful brown or gray. Similar homes were being built to the south in the West Adams area.

William, Henry, and Haynes decided the properties along Sixth and Seventh streets were more suitable for commercial buildings, hotels, and apartments. Good Samaritan Hospital was expanding from its location near the downtown area to Sixth Street, and hotels and apartment houses were already springing up in the blocks west of the hospital site. The city had followed Henry's recommendation and allowed cable car and electric trolley lines to be built on Sixth and Seventh. Henry had predicted the rise of the automobile, but in 1900, the lines would have to do as a means of transportation for west-side residents and visitors. The electric railway lines now linked Long Beach, Santa Monica, and San Bernardino to the city.

Passengers on the trolleys and cable cars were in effect a captive audience. Henry, William, and Haynes decided to take advantage of that fact. They formed the Los Angeles Billboard Company, and found soap, cigarette, and clothing companies to buy advertising. They paid artists to draw ads on large sheets of cardboard that could be placed on permanent billboards along the streets the men owned. The Wilshires also worked their California Club contacts for customers, and the company was nearly an immediate success.

Early billboard either on or near Wilshire Boulevard

Meanwhile, a group led by Tufts, the head of the City Council, started a golf club on Pico. As Henry had predicted, they named it the Los Angeles Country Club. Henry and William were charter members. Golf would be a source of personal pleasure as well as business contacts for the Wilshires. The two things Henry liked to do best was give speeches and play golf.

Although Henry was busy with his development and bill-board business, he found himself distracted by the latest political developments. Democratic leader William Jennings Bryan, who had sought the presidency in 1896 and was making another run at the 1900 election, had a large following in Los Angeles. From Henry's point of view, Bryan was a man to be admired, and he saw many similarities between them.

Bryan was born in Salem, Illinois, and Henry in Cincinnati, Ohio. Bryan was a liberal Democrat, Henry a Socialist. Bryan was called "the Great Commoner" because of his faith in the common people. Henry was called the Millionaire Socialist because he, too, sympathized with the workingman. Henry loved public speaking. Bryan had given 500 speeches in 1896, virtually inventing the political stump speech. His famous

"Cross of Gold" speech included the line: "You shall not press down upon the brow of labor this crown of thorns, you shall not crucify mankind upon a cross of gold." Henry could only wish the line were his own.

But they had differences as well. Bryan was an enemy of gold as the basis of the dollar and wanted the government to have closer control of the banks and railroads. Henry wanted the government to own the trusts and did not fully understand the issue of gold versus silver as the monetary standard. Bryan had been elected to Congress in 1890 and was a lawyer. Wilshire failed to graduate from Harvard and had not held elected office. Some people said Bryan was like the Platt River, two miles wide at the mouth and six inches deep. Wilshire was a reader and an intellectual.

William Jennings Bryan – "The Great Commoner"

If Henry were to become another William Jennings Bryan, he needed notoriety. He had taken some of his share of the profits from the billboard company and began to publish *The National-ist* again. He hit on a gimmick that could vault him onto the national scene: He decided to challenge Bryan to a debate. Although he and Bryan agreed on many things, Bryan had backed away from the idea of nationalizing the trusts. In reality, he did not understand many of the regulations that Congress was proposing to limit the trusts.

Henry learned that Bryan was coming to Los Angeles and sent him an invitation to debate. He offer to pay Bryan $5,000 the instant he stepped on stage and another $5,000 immediately after the debate. Bryan did not respond. Henry published the challenge in his newspaper and took out a full-page advertise-ment in the *Los Angeles Times.* He even tried to place an ad in Bryan's newspaper, *The Commoner,* but it was rejected as being "too personal."

After serving as a congressman from Nebraska, Bryan re-fused to run for any office lower than president of the United States. It was easy to see how he could ignore a challenge from a small-time Los Angeles socialist. His advisors told Bryan to simply ignore the challenge. Henry refused to be ignored and inferred that Bryan was afraid to debate him. He advertised in Bryan's town in Nebraska and went as far as posting signs across the street from Bryan's home. Nothing worked—but did Henry really expect results? Like Henry's runs for office, the challenge was a way to get his name and views before the public. He even changed the name of his paper from *The Nationalist* to *The Challenge.*

Wilshire decided he was on a roll. He looked for other ways to gain notoriety. He learned that the City Council was disgusted with the way people were abusing the new Sixth Street Park. Vagrants and dog walkers continued to litter the park, and loud, crackpot speakers were polluting the peace and quiet. The council passed an ordinance that prohibited speeches in public parks. Anyone violating the law would be arrested for disturbing the peace. Henry had found a cause.

He sent a letter to the chief of police telling of his intention to speak in the center of Sixth Street Park on November 20, 1900. He asked if the chief would not mind sending a large, threatening policeman to arrest him and if he could be taken away in a police wagon. The letter said he was a newspaperman and hoped the arrest would be helpful to circulation. "Any stick will do when you need to beat a dog, and my arrest will serve to beat the dog of circulation for my weekly paper," the letter said. Henry also published a front-page article in *The Challenge* publicizing his intentions and his series of articles on free speech in America. He notified the *Los Angeles Times* as well.

Wilshire gave the speech in November to three vagrants and two dogs. He showed up in tan shoes, a soft, brown hat, and a light suit with the trousers rolled up at the bottom. A policeman showed up and arrested Henry, then directed him to a horse-drawn police carriage at the curb. Henry was charged with disturbing the peace. The judge levied a fine and let him go with a warning. The judge said free speech would always trump a city ordinance. But he also informed Henry that he could have given his speech without incident if he had obtained a permit from City Hall.

Wilshire wrote a scathing front-page article claiming the capitalist press and private corporations were making a mockery of the First Amendment. No permit should be required for an American to express his or her views in public. It had been suggested that if he wanted to give a speech he should have rented a hall, the article said. He explained that he was fortunate enough to do so but that many people were not. "Should economic circumstances deprive a citizen from the right of free speech and free assembly?" Henry wrote.

The *Los Angeles Times* had sent a reporter to the park as Henry had hoped. The next day an article appeared with the headline "Wilshire Wins Out in Court, Public Speaking in Parks Is Lawful, Ordinance Forbidding It Null and Void." Henry had won his battle. Surely it would be regarded as his "Cross of Gold" speech. It turned out that the *Times* also published some facetious articles under the heading "H. Gaylord Blossoms," "Pulled for Blowing Off in the Park, Much Wind Soughed Through the Trees," and "Ecstatic Patrol-Wagon Rode for the Philosopher-Puts Up Bail." He had not intended to be ridiculed, but publicity was publicity.

The socialist party in Los Angeles approached Henry about running again for Congress in the Sixth Congressional District. He campaigned and lost. But as always, Henry's view was that even a loss was a victory because he had advanced the cause.

By 1901, Henry had tired of Los Angeles and his business interests. William could develop the real estate on his own, and

Haynes could hire someone to administer the billboard business. He missed New York City. He decided to move back and take *The Challenge* with him. New York City was the center of socialism in America, and that was where he belonged.

PRICE, 5 CENTS
WILSHIRE'S
"LET THE NATION OWN THE TRUSTS"
MARCH, 1908
GOD KNOWS
WHAT SHALL A MAN DO WHO IS STARVING AND CANNOT FIND WORK?
PRIVATE PROPERTY
TAFT SPHINX
CAPITALISTIC DESERT
CONSULTING THE ORACLE

WILSHIRE'S MAGAZINE
200 William St. New York

CHAPTER 6
How to Lose a Fortune in Publishing

While running for Congress, Henry became acutely aware of how fractured the socialist movement was in America. The Socialist Labor Party consisted mostly of German immigrants, and there were many who thought the members were not really American. Henry George's single tax idea was attractive to the middle class and the skilled wage earners but not to many trade unions. The American Federation of Labor, founded in 1886, changed the playing field of socialism in America. Henry's California supporters were mostly Fabian socialists who believed capitalism could be saved through the normal political process. They were only a little bit Marxist, which Henry compared to being a little bit pregnant. Still, Henry heartily agreed with one tenet of the philosophy: The Fabians believed you had to win people's hearts and minds for the movement to be successful. The influence of the written word was the best way to influence what happened at the ballot box. Henry pledged his fortune and his efforts to that ideal.

Henry's good friend Dr. John R. Haynes was working closely with the Union Reform League in Los Angeles. The League's platform, similar to that of the new Socialist Labor Party, called for nationalizing all public services, rapidly increasing land taxation, imposing income and inheritance taxes, allowing government to issue currency without interference from the banks, establishing postal savings banks, and granting women's suffrage. It also agitated for prohibiting child labor, creating compulsory accident insurance, and creating a social safety net.

By 1900 Wilshire's small socialist weekly, *The Challenge*, was one of many socialist journals reflecting the views of the Union's various camps. The *International Socialist Review*, edited by A.M. Simons, was another. Simons, who was more intellectual than Wilshire, wrote a history of the United States within the framework of Marxist analysis. But many publications went bankrupt due to lack of subscribers, including *The Coming Nation*, *The American Fabian*, *The Social Economist*, and *The Coming Light*. Some of the newer journals like *The Socialist Review* and the *Bellamy Review* were barely hanging on. Unlike these journals, *The Challenge* had a rich man for a publisher. Unfortunately Henry knew nothing about the publishing business, but a lack of expertise had never stopped him. Henry needed a platform for his ideas and those of leading American socialists. He also required well-known contributors to attract a widespread audience. Henry knew the best and most liberal writers were in New York City.

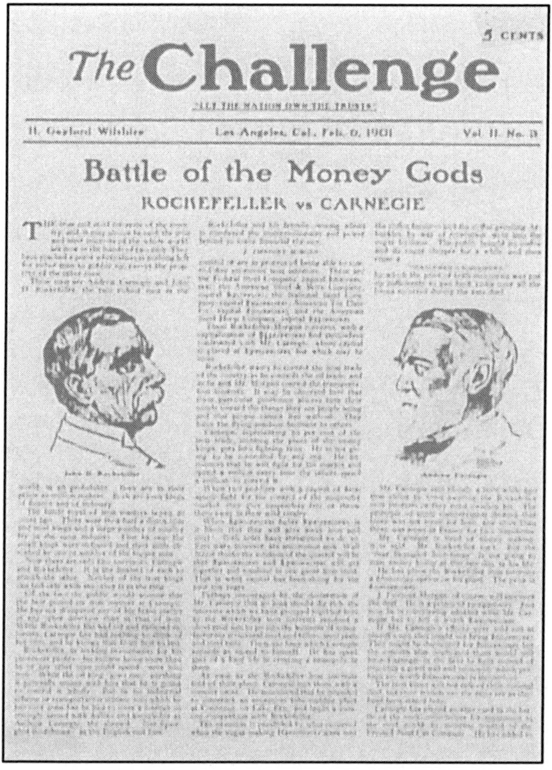

Charles E. Young Research Library - UCLA
MOBILE MAGAZINE: *Henry moved The Challenge from Los Angeles to New York to Toronto and back to New York, all in a two-year period.*

Henry put Haynes in charge of the billboard business and William in charge of selling their remaining lots, and he took the train to New York City. Henry rented a small office on Second Avenue and notified every New York socialist he knew that he was open for business and would appreciate their support. Henry was sorry his old friend Henry George had died of a stroke in 1897; he could have used his counsel and contacts. Daniel De Leon was still in New York but had grown unpopular.

At the time, a bitter struggle was taking place between Samuel Gompers and Eugene Debs for control of the nation's left. Gompers represented the American labor movement and Debs the new American Socialist Party, composed of the Social Reform Union, the National Christian Citizenship League, the American Fabian League, and the Union Reform League. The more radical Debs believed craft unions like Gompers' AFL were too weak to go up against big business. Gompers believed labor unions should focus on improving working conditions through collective bargaining rather than political organizing.

Long, lean, and bald, Debs had kind eyes and a love for alcohol. He was a prophet more respected than followed. Like Bliss and his supporters, Debs believed the movement would be stronger if left-leaning groups—though part of a larger alliance—pursued their own causes. During the party's first formal convention, held in March 1900 in New York City, suspicion, vituperation, jealousy, and the desire for power seemed to trump ideology. The atmosphere reeked of class-conscious radicalism and soapbox oratory as to what Marx did or did not advocate. After a great deal of squabbling, vote-taking, arm-twisting and name-calling, a strong Social Democratic Party won out.

BATTLE FOR THE LEFT: *Samuel Gompers, left, and Eugene Debs, right, were at odds over how to improve the lives of the working class. Gompers believed unions should improve conditions through collective bargaining, while Debs thought the unions should be politically active.*

By the summer of 1900, the nation had one Socialist Labor Party and two Social Democratic Parties, one with headquarters in Chicago and the other in Springfield. All three segments supported the same platform and ticket: Debs for president and Job Harriman for vice president. Despite his personal philosophy, Debs worked hard to unify all the groups. "Let us dismiss all minor considerations and unite … in one mighty effort to hasten the end of capitalism and the inauguration of the co-operative commonwealth," he said. During the campaign, Debs railed against private means of production and argued passionately for political equality, economic freedom, and social progress—issues he said the two major parties routinely ignored. The Republican Party was riding on the coattails of the current economic prosperity and its ability to preserve it. The

Democratic Party, relying on support from the urban working class, was arguing for economic and social stability.

William Randolph Hearst was promoting Democrat William Jennings Bryan in the pages of his newspapers. Though publishers often used their papers as a political tool, Hearst was perfecting the practice. He had purchased *The San Francisco Examiner* and *The New York Journal,* and was considering starting a newspaper in Los Angeles that he intended to call *The Los Angeles Examiner.* Hearst favored a mild form of collectivism and espoused municipal ownership of public utilities, and many feared he was a socialist. He was a Democrat, but in reality his views were mostly his own. He has been accused of using his newspapers to influence public and political opinion to the extent that he used altered facts to create an event. There are some who say the Hearst papers actually started the Spanish-American War. The name "yellow journalism" is sometimes used to describe the use of newspapers to create events.

Not only did Hearst back Bryan but he also asked Debs to drop out of the race. A ballot cast for Debs and Harriman was a wasted vote, he said. Debs replied, "Comrade Hearst, the Party has chosen Job Harriman and me for their candidates for Vice-President and President respectively of the Social Democratic Party. We shall stand as such candidates to be voted upon on election day, all reports and rumors to the contrary notwithstanding." Hearst intimated in his papers that the Republican Party was financially underwriting Debs and Harriman as a way to split the liberal vote. Henry suspected Hearst was right. William McKinley, the Republican incumbent, won in a landslide.

WILLIAM RANDOLPH HEARST: *The publisher backed Democrat William Jennings Bryan in the 1900 presidential race and urged socialist Eugene Debs to drop out of the race. In the end Republican William McKinley remained in the Oval Office.*

Henry was becoming more radical now that he was living in New York, which was reflected in the pages of *The Challenge*. He did not lean as far left as his ex-wife Hannah, but he came to believe that a great economic revolution was about to occur. One minister in New York City likened Wilshire, Simons, and other socialist left-wingers to the millenarians who had disposed of their possessions to prepare for the Second Coming of Christ. As Henry poured more and more money into *The Challenge,* he did seem hell-bent on bankrupting himself.

His front-page editorial in December 1900 stated,

"This journal has been given life in order to voice for this community certain thoughts and ideas of a radical nature that are either suppressed altogether in the daily press or are published in such a desultory manner that those in sympathy with such thought suffer from lack of continuity. ... We believe that society is approaching its critical point and that a transformation must ensue—that the present competitive system, embracing the private ownership of capital, to a shell which protects the formation of a new and better society within itself. When this new society is ready it will burst its shell and step forth, fully formed and complete."

About this time the nation was in the throes of anti-socialism due to the growth of the Industrial Workers of the World, known variously as the IWW or the Wobblies. The IWW rose out of the terrible strikes in 1903-1904 in the gold fields of Cripple Creek, Colorado. The IWW became one of the most authentic revolutionary groups in the American labor movement. One its leaders, William Dudley Haywood, known as Big Bill Haywood, was accused of helping to assassinate the former governor of Idaho. He was acquitted, but socialists and the labor movement had a bad name in 1901. *The Challenge* had defended Haywood in several issues. The assassination of President McKinley in 1901 by an anarchist did not help the public attitude toward communists, anarchists, and fellow travelers. Despite the suspicion of many, however, the Socialist Party in America grew dramatically during the next ten years.

When Wilshire moved *The Challenge* from Los Angeles to New York, he had to apply for a new postal permit. He sought to mail his paper as second-class matter, the usual rate for newspapers and magazines. However, Third Assistant Postmaster General Edwin Madden rejected the application. No reason was given.

This meant postage for *The Challenge* would cost $300 a week instead of $30. This was prohibitively expensive, even for a man as wealthy as Wilshire. He appealed, and Madden replied that he had refused the normal rate because the paper advertised Wilshire's lectures and causes. Wilshire wrote back, arguing that it was not his custom to advertise his lectures and that he did not intend to do so in the future. General Madden replied that a paper advertising ideas belonged in the same class as one that advertises soap; therefore, he could not classify the paper as second-class mail. Madden informed Henry that he would reconsider if Henry stopped pontificating in *The Challenge*'s pages. It was obvious to Wilshire that he had an enemy in the Post Office.

The only way to maintain *The Challenge* as a platform for his ideas was to move. Henry investigated publishing in London, Paris, or Berlin. All were too expensive and too distant from his American audience. He had always admired Canada's socialist movement; it was more Fabian in its principles than the Socialist Democratic Party was. In addition, Toronto was close to Ohio and the heart of industrial America. With industry came labor and lots of readers. Henry decided to relocate *The Challenge* to Canada. He also decided he could produce a more attractive publication if he converted *The Challenge* from a weekly to a monthly magazine. He moved to Toronto in 1901 and began publishing his namesake monthly, *Wilshire's Magazine*. The last issue of *The Challenge* was published on July 10, 1901.

Henry looked to other magazines for examples of successful formats. One of his favorites was *McClure's Magazine*. It was more of a progressive journal than a socialist publication. It featured articles by investigative journalists that Teddy Roosevelt called "muckrakers" because they wrote about the poorest levels of society. *McClure's* authors like Lincoln Steffens, Ida Tarbell, Samuel Hopkins Adams, and David Graham Phillips were well-known to many literate Americans. The magazine was printed in color on quality paper. It published cartoons, an opinion page, and articles about crime and corruption, child labor, patent medicines, cleanliness in the meat-packing industry, fraud and waste, public health and safety, and illegal financial practices. Wilshire thought *McClure's Magazine* should be hailed as a public service. S.S. McClure, the owner and publisher, rejected the use of "yellow journalism" to sell magazines. He chose instead to tell the truth.

TRUTH TELLER: *McClure's Magazine, a progressive monthly, is credited with creating muckraking journalism. Among its most famous articles was Ida Tarbell's series on Standard Oil.*

Taking a page from *McClure's*, Henry realized that controversy was one of the best ways to stimulate interest in his new magazine. In the magazine's early months, it told both sides of an issue to stimulate interest. There was a belief toward the end of the nineteenth century that Charles Darwin's doctrine could be applied to business practices. Herbert Spencer, a follower of Darwin who coined the term "survival of the fittest," preached an "equilibration mechanism principle," which swept through business circles in the early twentieth century. Spencer saw life as a struggle among individuals, and so intense was his view that he was in effect a philosophical anarchist. He believed that human relations must be governed by natural law and that the state should function only as an occasional umpire. He vehemently opposed forcibly burdening the superior (the successful) to support the inferior (the unsuccessful).

Businessmen easily accepted Spencer's version of what would become known as social Darwinism. Even religious leaders got into the act. The bishop of Massachusetts proclaimed, "In the long run it is only to the man of morality that wealth comes. ... Godliness is in league with riches." William Graham Sumner, a professor at Yale and a former clergyman, said, "This is a world in which the rule is 'Root, Hog, or Die,' and it is also a world in which 'the longest pole knocks down the most persimmons.' Self-interest does and should rule, and there pessimism should be no chains on enterprise – nor any aids such as the protective tariff. The only law was that of the survival of the fittest: liberty lay solely in the right to struggle." The social Darwinists believed that philanthropists would take care of the poor, blind, and aged. A prosperous economy that created good jobs would lift all boats, they argued. Any interference by government, including taxes on the wealthy, disrupted the natural system.

The social Darwinists were a ready foil for *Wilshire's Magazine.* During the first few years of the magazine, articles by Leon Trotsky, Oscar Wilde, Jack London, and Upton Sinclair could be found in the pages of *Wilshire's Magazine.* Two years after its founding, the magazine was the leading socialist publication in America, with circulation exceeding 100,000.

UCLA Charles E. Young Research Library
Early edition of Wilshire's Magazine

Henry and Sinclair became fast friends. Sinclair, who Henry called "Uppie," was a freelance writer who grew up poor in the rural south. His father was a liquor salesman and an alcoholic—the reason Sinclair was a teetotaler. As a part-time reporter for the magazine *Appeal to Reason,* he wrote several articles about the meatpacking industry. He found the working conditions as well as the sanitary conditions deplorable. His articles received national attention, and *Appeal to Reason* sent him to Chicago to get a close look at the industry. Sinclair worked undercover for seven weeks and slept in a settlement house near the meatpacking plant. He talked to social workers, laborers, workers' relatives, and the unemployed. Besides the articles for *Appeal to Reason,* Sinclair was writing a book about the meatpacking industry called *The Jungle,* though he doubted anyone would publish it. Sinclair was an ideal writer for *Wilshire's Magazine,* and his articles took on social Darwinism with biting reportage. Henry paid Sinclair as much as he could afford.

Library of Congress Photo
MUCKRAKING AT ITS FINEST: *Upton Sinclair spent seven weeks working undercover in a Chicago meatpacking plant, which he documented in his book The Jungle.*

Sinclair lacked humor but made up for it in sincerity. He had genuine empathy for working-class people and fought for their betterment all his life. He wrote movingly about their poverty in several *Wilshire's Magazine* articles. Wilshire included sections from the Sinclair's classic *The Jungle* in the magazine as well as other quotes from Sinclair.

"It is difficult to get a man to understand something when his job depends on not understanding it."

"All day long this man would toil thus, his whole being centered upon the purpose of making twenty-three instead of twenty-two and a half cents an hour; and then his product would be reckoned up by the census taker, and jubilant captains of industry would boast of it in their banquet halls, telling how our workers are nearly twice as efficient as those of any other country. If we are the greatest nation the sun ever shone upon, it would seem to be mainly because we have been able to goad our wage-earners to this pitch of frenzy."

"Man is an evasive beast, given to cultivating strange notions about himself. He is humiliated by his simian ancestry, and tries to deny his animal nature, to persuade himself that he is not limited by its weaknesses nor concerned in its fate. And this impulse may be harmless, when it is genuine. But what are we to say when we see the formulas of heroic self-deception made use of by unheroic self-indulgence?"

Henry and "Uppie" kept up a lively correspondence over the years. They frequently were critical of the socialist party and how hidebound and timid the socialist press had become. As they became older they both became more in support of syndicalism and the trade unions as a way to bring about change.

***

In Jack London, Henry found a livelier companion than Sinclair. Henry and Sinclair met London in the bar of a hotel where the American Socialist Party was meeting in June 1901.

"Henry, who is the loudmouth over by the bar? Everyone seems to know him," Sinclair asked.

"I don't know. Handsome devil, isn't he? I think half the women in the room are looking at him."

The large, dark-haired young man saw them looking at him and walked across the room to where they were sitting.

"Do I know you two? Or more to the point, should I know you?"

"My name is Upton Sinclair, and this is Gaylord Wilshire. We have not met. However, a man as drunk and loud as you are should not go unintroduced."

"I am not drunk, but I do like to be heard. Not like these lily-livered socialists on the platform, afraid of their own shadow. Now that you mention it, perhaps I should get drunk. How about I buy you two fellows a drink? What will you have?"

Henry said, "My friend here only drinks sarsaparilla. But I will have a drink with you as long as you let me buy the first round. I don't like to drink with strangers. What did you say your name was?"

"Jack London from Oakland, California. I am known as the King of the Oyster Pirates."

Henry said, "I know about oystermen. I used to live in San Francisco. A pretty wild bunch. I also know Oakland, a lovely small town. I landed there once."

"You are looking at the future mayor of Oakland if I have my way," London replied.

Sinclair commented, "Good for you. We need socialist mayors. I ran for Congress once. I enjoyed it immensely. What do you do for a living, Jack?"

"I am a writer or so I like to believe. I majored in English at the University of California at Berkeley after my adventures as a seaman. I worked the gold mines in the Klondike and eschewed work as a tramp in California. Great fodder for a writer. I have sold a few magazine stories and have a novel about Alaska and a wolf that *The Saturday Evening Post* is thinking of buying."

"We are writers as well," Henry said. "Sinclair is a journalist, and I own a small magazine that I intend to turn into the largest socialist journal in the country. Have you ever written about the trials of the working class? I might be interested in buying one of your stories, though my magazine is just getting started and I cannot pay much."

"I am always interested in selling my stories. Remarkable, just remarkable. I meet two fellows in a bar, and one of them offers to buy my work. Wait, did you say your name was

Wilshire? Are you the Millionaire Socialist who owns *The Challenge*? I like that little blurb."

"I did own it, but thanks to a pig at the Post Office, it went under. Now I publish *Wilshire's Magazine* out of Toronto. Tell me, Jack, how serious are you about the cause?"

"Socialism is my passion. It is like a lover, warming me when I am cold. No woman, at least at the moment, fills me with as much desire. Henry, I would be most interested in submitting two short stories that might be of interest to your magazine. One is called "The Tramp" and the other is "People of the Abyss." Give me your address, and I will send them to you. What do you pay?"

"It depends on the length. Let me see them, and I will give you a price."

"Fair enough," London said.

Young Jack London

Henry's relationship with London—both personal and professional—lasted many years. His writing was popular with socialists. The Russians in particular adored him, and Emma Goldman called him the only truly revolutionary author in America. Wilshire published "The Tramp," which focused on London's experiences with Kelly's Army in California, a protest over unemployment. He also printed parts of "People of the Abyss," which focused on working conditions in London. It reads in part:

"The workhouses have no space left in which to pack the starving crowds who are craving every day and night at their doors for food and shelter. All the charitable institutions have exhausted their means in trying to raise supplies of food for the famishing residents of the garrets and cellars of London lanes and alleys. The quarters of the Salvation Army in various parts of London are nightly besieged by hosts of the unemployed and the hungry for whom neither shelter nor the means of sustenance can be provided. It has been urged that the criticism I have passed on things as they are in England is too pessimistic. I must say, in extenuation, that of optimists I am the most optimistic. But I measure manhood less by political aggregations than by individuals. Society grows, while political machines rack to pieces and become 'scrap.' For the English, so far as manhood and womanhood and health and happiness go, I see a broad and smiling future. But for a great deal of the political

machinery, which at present mismanages for them, I see noth-ing else than the scrap heap."

Henry had trouble paying his authors from the beginning. In November, 1902 he wrote Jack London about his financial problems with *Wilshire's Magazine*:

"Dear London,

'The People of the Abyss' is estimated at 60,000 words, and we were to take it at a cent a word for what we used. As I told you, at the time the arrangement was made, I was very hard up and was not sure what I could do with it, but would do the best possible. We have been laboring under tremendous expenses and heavy losses, and I hardly know how the thing is coming out, although matters are looking considerable better today as I am about to make great economies in the management and in the production.

'The People of the Abyss' is a great work and has certainly done us a great deal of good, but it looks as if you can put very fine stuff in a socialist magazine but the money that comes in from it doesn't amount to much of anything, the socialists being so few in number. We have omitted Chapters 12 and 17 and part of another, making altogether 5,300 words omitted, that is, 543,700 used, making a total of $537 that we owe you altogeth-er. Of this we have already paid you $132, and enclose here-with a check for $205, leaving a balance of $200 still due, which we will forward when we have run the whole book."

London needed money in 1903 and asked Wilshire to pay him for the articles he had submitted as per their financial agreement. Henry wrote back in January of 1903,

"I feel I should further explain my position to you. I would say at once that I have put in something like $75,000 in cash into my magazine, and it has practically stripped me of every dollar that we can raise, and it is still running behind; and now I am at my wits end to get money to keep it going."

Later in August of 1906 Henry had other plans for paying London.

"Under separate cover I am sending you a copy of a prospectus of a gold mine which I have become interested in and which I think is the finest thing that ever developed in my mining experience in California. You know I was interested in mining for a number of years there and am more or less familiar with them. I don't expect to sell you any stock although I am sure it would be a good purchase for you but I would like it if it just the same to you, to let me liquidate that old debt that I owe you for 'The Abyss' and some other stuff you sent me by giving you $200 in this mining stock. We are going to put the price up to double what it is now and I have no question at all that if the mine comes out anywhere near where we think it will be worth many times the stock I am sending you."

Despite the financial problems between London, Wilshire, and Sinclair they remained friends for many years. Their love of socialism and mutual friends kept them close. Both Sinclair and London submitted pieces to *Wilshire's Magazine* over the years. They critiqued each others work and spent time with each other when they could. They became friends with each others' families and friends. Henry was glad when London married Charmian Kittredge. He congratulated him on his choice. They kept track of each other's families, health, publications and projects. Henry wrote London in January, 1909,

"We were so distressed to get Charmian's letter to Mary of December, from Sydney, stating you were sick, and that 'The Snark' would have to be sold and the trip given up…. I have a letter from Sinclair, stating that you have signed his Peace Manifesto. The only other names, apparently, are those of C.E. Russell, reverend John D. Long and George Sterling. All the rest of us have refused to sign, for one reason or another. I don't see how he ever got you to sign it so quickly. His play in San Francisco seems to have been a failure, from what Meta told us last night, but he expects to revise it and bring it out in good shape later on. Hope springs eternal in Uppie's breast.

"Bernard Shaw has been reported sick, but apparently it was somewhat exaggerated, as Shaw tells the reporters he is not sick, but dead."

The truth was the three men needed each other. Henry sought writers and inspiration. Sinclair required money and emotional support. And London had lots of friends but needed socialist companions who understood and shared his views. London encouraged Sinclair to complete *The Jungle*, which he called a great testimonial for the socialist cause, and recommended the book to his publisher. Similarly, Sinclair gave London emotional support and encouraged him to stop drinking and lead a more moral life. "A man who does not drink cannot be trusted," London said, but he seemed to trust Sinclair anyway. It was not uncommon to see the three men together at socialist gatherings. One socialist said they seemed inseparable at times.

Wilshire's Magazine was selling but was still not a profitable proposition. Wilshire needed to bring the magazine back to the States. He wrote the postmaster general a letter saying he could mail his magazine from Canada at half the cost of mailing it from the United States. The Postal Service eventually replied that he could obtain a second-class permit if he returned to the United States. It was a small battle, but he had won.

In late 1901 the Socialist Party of Canada asked Henry to run for Parliament in the 1902 election. Henry had applied for Canadian citizenship the previous year and was now a citizen of the United States, Great Britain, and Canada. He agreed to run but withdrew because he decided to return to New York City.

No sooner had he returned to New York than the Social Democratic Party asked him to run for Congress in the Tenth Congressional District of Manhattan. He could not refuse. He intended to use running for office as a way to expand circulation with the goal of securing 250,000 subscribers. He owed money to many of his authors, including London and Sinclair. He began to include contests and lotteries for pianos and small orange groves in California. He took virtually any advertisement that came his way to bring in revenue. Still, the magazine was barely hanging on, and Henry was forced to dip further into his savings and investments.

UCLA Charles E. Young Research Library

One of the best things that ever happened to Henry occurred in the summer of 1904. He met Mary McReynolds, an artist and social worker from Illinois who was twenty years his junior, at a meeting of the Social Democratic Party. She was pretty, relaxed, and soft-spoken. Her presence helped calm Henry. He was the dreamer; she was the common sense. She shared Henry's passion for socialism and helped form the Women's National Progressive League. Mary was so different from Hannah. Hannah was simplistic in her violent views about capitalism where Mary believed as Henry did that capitalism could be saved if the citizens were well informed. Hannah had no real interest in helping others as individuals. Mary was just the opposite. She genuinely cared about other people and her listening ability made her many lifelong friends. The attraction between Henry and Mary McReynolds was immediate, and the romance quickly turned serious. They married on February 6, 1904. Henry's best friend, Julian Hawthorne, the son of author Nathaniel Hawthorne, served as best man. Julian had lived next door to Henry when he lived in New York and became his best friend for many years. He had no better friend, however, than Mary McReynolds.

MR. AND MRS. WILSHIRE: *Mary McReynolds, shown with Henry soon after their marriage in 1904, was a calming influence on her new husband. Also a socialist, she helped form the Women's National Progressive League and was the first psychoanalyst to practice in Los Angeles.*

By the summer of 1904, the magazine was deep in debt. The circulation declined despite the many attempts of offering prizes for those who solicited the most subscriptions. Print costs rose, and more and more authors wanted to be paid for their writing. Mailing costs were a constant drain on the balance sheet of the magazine. It was apparent that one way to increase income was to raise the price of the publication. Five cents a copy was nearly giving the periodical away. Mc Clures was selling for fifteen cents a copy. Henry insisted that the magazine should be able to be purchased by the poor and kept the price down despite the threat of bankruptcy. He increased the amount of advertising which helped but not enough. Wilshire needed a way to rescue it. Then he remembered the Lost Creek Gold Mine. Henry believed he was destined to become a key figure in the socialist party. He needed a way to make that happen. He and Mary always joked about needing to find gold. Perhaps that was not so far-fetched. He wrote to his old friend Clarence and asked about the mine. Perhaps his destiny could be found in Bishop Creek.

CARDINAL MINE AS IT APPEARED IN 1920.
OVER $1,500,000 IN GOLD WAS TAKEN FROM
THIS MINE FROM 1920 TO 1937.
Ken Stroman.

CHAPTER 7
Everyone Needs a Gold Mine

enry was running out of money fast. *Wilshire's Magazine* was popular but not profitable enough to pay the writers regularly, so London, Sinclair, Shaw, and other writers began selling their articles elsewhere. It was understandable since many of them were spendthrifts. London drank most of his royalties as fast as they came in. Sinclair, like Wilshire, spent most of his on socialist causes. Shaw lived the life of a wealthy Londoner and now wanted to be paid prior to publication. His literary agent insisted that Shaw be paid large sums for even the smallest of articles.

Without these big names, circulation lagged. Henry knew his editorials were becoming repetitive and boring. He tried to spice up the magazine with cartoons, jokes, poetry, and prizes for persons who got the most subscriptions. Prizes included a fine large automobile, three elegant pianos, a piano player, two self-playing organs, phonographs, cameras, bicycles, watches, china, billiard tables, typewriters, and at one point a ten-acre fruit ranch in Ontario, California. He paid off on the prizes but had difficulty explaining to himself and his bookkeeper how he could afford these premiums. Still, nothing seemed to work. He is needed income to support his wife as well as his magazine.

Henry had read that the Homestake Gold Mine in Lead, South Dakota, was producing $10,000 worth of gold a month.

Reading about the Homestake reminded Henry about his friend Clarence and the Lost Creek Gold Mine in Bishop, California. He wondered if Clarence and his father still owned the mine. Did they ever manage to capitalize the stock? Were they still interested in taking on a partner?

Henry rummaged through his Harvard memorabilia and found Clarence's home address. It was now 1905, and he hoped the address was still valid after all these years. He wrote a letter asking about the mine and a potential partnership. He also heard from friends that two mines in British Guiana were for sale, the Tassawini Gold Mine and the Aremu Gold Mine. He wrote for a prospectus on the British Guiana mines as well. He had very little money to invest but knew he could rely on his salesmanship to find interested partners.

Two weeks after sending the letter, Henry received a long reply from Clarence that said they had sold their shares and claims and the Lost Creek Gold Mine was now part of the Bishop Creek Gold Mining Company's claim. Two prospector brothers from Lone Pine, Felix and Charles Myerson, had found gold near the headwaters of the middle fork of Bishop Creek. They staked a claim and called it the Tip Top Mine. They worked it until 1895 and then sold it to a group of investors from New York City. The investors called their company the Bishop Creek Gold Company, and the mine became the Bishop Creek Gold Mine. The company started a limited mining operation and a small tent village. The New York company engaged in some mining while going through various stages of organization. On February 16, 1905, the company decided to go public, and the value of the stock was placed at $5 million. Clarence stated in his letter that the owners were interested in selling the mine.

Henry decided he needed to visit the mine personally before making any investment. A trip would satisfy his own due diligence and allow him to describe the mine to others should he decide to take on partners. The magazine's survival was too important to rely on hearsay. He must see the mine for himself.

The mine, described in the stock prospectus, was 18 miles southwest of Bishop in Inyo County, California, at an altitude of almost 8,500 feet. It was near Mount Emerson, one of the taller mountains in the Sierra Nevada at 13,225 feet. The large Lake Sabrina was less than a mile from the mine, and other streams and a small river were nearby. The only means of transportation was horse and wagon.

Henry left the East Coast on May 23, 1906, taking the Union Pacific Railway to Chicago, then the Atchison, Topeka and the Santa Fe to the small town of Barstow, California. The train ride through the Rocky Mountains was spectacular. He particularly enjoyed the immense Mojave Desert that included Death Valley. Death Valley was strange, beautiful, and a little frightening. It was so big and so void of any apparent life. He spent the night in Barstow and waited to catch a stagecoach to Keeler, where you could take the small narrow gauge Carson and Colorado Railway north to Laws, a small town about four miles from the larger town of Bishop. In Bishop, he would meet the mining engineer in charge of the Bishop Creek Gold Mine. The owners of the mine had been only too happy to provide information and contacts to a prospective buyer. It was new and exciting to Henry. It felt like a real adventure.

The stagecoach to Keeler was especially enjoyable to Henry, like something out of the old frontier days. When he got to Keeler, he spent the night in a small hotel with just four guest rooms and a small bar that doubled as a restaurant. The train arrived early in the morning.

LOCAL LOCOMOTIVE: This narrow gauge locomotive was used by the Carson and Colorado Railway, which traveled a mere 300 miles between Keeler, California, and Mound House, Nevada. The C& C Railroad was sold to the Southern Pacific Railroad in 1900 and became a branch of the larger railway.

The train had only one passenger car and seven loaded freight cars. This was going to be another adventure. The passenger cars had wooden benches that faced forward. There was no glass in the windows, and the dusty desert winds blew in freely. The little locomotive huffed and puffed its way up the inclines. The train was slow by 1905 standards but seemed safe and reliable. Henry found the scenery even more beautiful than the Rockies because of the steep ascent from the desert to the Sierra Nevada. The reddish-brown earth of the desert morphed into green grass along the Owens River, then became rocky foothills that turned into majestic mountains. The white clouds that hugged the snow-capped peaks made Henry wish he had a camera.

When the train stopped in Lone Pine to load coal and water, Henry paid a penny to look through a telescope at Mount Whitney, the highest peak in the continental United States at 14,505 feet. The mountain range was the most beautiful thing Henry had ever seen, and he was pleased that he could tell his friends he had seen Mount Whitney firsthand. Spring wildflowers dotted the hills above Lone Pine, and aspens and pines had sprouted up wherever there was water. Lone Pine wasn't much of a town, but it was clean and quaint.

Henry met a miner on the train who told him stories about the prospectors and ranchers who had first come to the Owens Valley and the High Sierra. The old miner said many of the original settlers were Spanish and Australian sheep ranchers. They built ranch houses and brought sheep to graze on the valley's rich grasses. When the Gold Rush hit, it brought hundreds of prospectors. Many miners who had failed on the west side of the Sierra came to the eastern side. Some found gold but in small amounts. They were convinced that thick veins of gold were buried in the rock formations, but heavy machinery and lots of water would be required to mine it. The cost of extracting the gold would likely exceed its value, he said. Only rich mining companies would be able to tap the treasure, the old-timer told him. "That is exactly why I am here," Henry thought to himself. "I want to head one of those rich mining companies."

When Henry arrived in Laws six hours after leaving Lone Pine, he found a neat depot, an agent's house, a section boss's house, outhouses, a water tank, and an engine turntable. He also saw several cabins, barns, and corrals as well as a thriving business district with two general stores, a small hotel, restaurant, boarding house, pool hall, dance hall, blacksmith shop, post office, barber shop, gunpowder magazine, and large warehouse. It was a small, busy town full of life. He liked it immediately.

LAWS STATION: Before Henry built cabins for the families of his Bishop Creek workers, his miners had to go to Laws to see their wives and children, costing the company untold man hours.

Henry was met at the depot by the mining engineer, named Steiner. He was a tall, muscular man who wore a long-handled gray mustache. He shook Henry's hand and welcomed him to Laws. He asked if Henry would like something to drink, but Henry was anxious to see the mine. Steiner said the mine was about a nine-hour ride on horseback from Laws so they would wait until the next day to make the trip. He had taken a room for Henry at the hotel across the street. Steiner said the food was good at the hotel—as was the beer. Henry laughed and said both the beer and the bed would be most welcome.

After a good night's sleep, Henry met Steiner in the cafe. Henry sat down at a round wooden table and was served the largest pancake he had ever seen, four eggs, a slab of bacon, and coffee. Henry was not used to eating such a large breakfast and was forced to loosen his belt a notch.

As they ate, Steiner made conversation. "I was wondering, Mr. Wilshire, just how much you know about gold mining."

"Very little, I am afraid," Henry said. "My father once owned a steel mill, and I worked there for a period of time. I didn't know anything about making steel either, but I assure you I am a quick study. An old miner I met on the train told me there is very little gold to be found in the streams anymore but that there are veins of gold buried in the mountains. He said it requires lots of money and machinery to get it out, and the cost of extracting the gold often exceeds its value. Is that true?"

"Yes and no," Steiner replied. "It depends on the quality of the gold and size of the vein you hit. There are mines that have paid their owners millions of dollars, and there are mines that barely paid the miners' wages. I need to tell you up front, Mr. Wilshire, that gold mining is a gamble. It is not a get-rich-quick proposal. The days of the Gold Rush are over."

"That much I know. I have done a great deal of reading about various mines that hit it big. There is not much written about mines that failed, but I assume there are more failures than successes."

"That is true. I don't want you to think I am being a braggart when I say I am one of the best mining engineers in the area. Bishop Creek Gold Mine is a fortune waiting to happen for the right owner."

"I hope I am that owner. You come highly recommended, Mr. Steiner. I have come here to see for myself what I might be getting into if I decide to invest in the mine. I hope you will be candid and patient with my ignorant questions."

"I would not respect a man who did not want to come and see for himself what he was investing in. As for your questions, I assure you no question is ignorant, though the answers sometimes are. Fire away, and I will try my best to answer them truthfully."

"My first question is about the railroad on which I arrived. Is it the only means of transportation to Laws? And how far is Laws from the mine?"

"The C&C is not the only means of transportation, but it is the best. Some people say the C&C Railroad is a 300-mile track to nowhere, but that is not true. I have found it a reliable little railroad capable of transporting heavy cargo from Barstow. It looks a little like a toy train, doesn't it? But I assure you it does the job. If the mine is to develop, we are going to need heavy machinery, so you are smart to ask about the railroad. In answer to your second question, the mine is eighteen miles west of here. The road is not paved and climbs up a 5,000-foot grade. We use twenty-mule teams to pull heavy loads up to the mine. You will notice hundreds of mules outside town. That is because mules are our main means of transportation up here."

"I noticed the mules as we approached Laws on the train. I was wondering why there were more mules than horses."

"A good mule is worth three horses when it comes to pulling a load. Oxen are good as well, but mules are better."

"I am impressed with Laws. It seems a nice small town and rather new, is it not?"

"Most of it has been built in the last five years. The hotel is a little older, but the station house was built last year. I live here when I am not up at the mine. We have a tent camp and a meat house up there, but tents will not suffice in the coldest months. We pretty much shut down the mine in the winter."

"If you had cabins up there, could you operate the mine longer?" Henry asked.

"Mr. Wilshire, I already like the way you think. If we had cabins, we could probably work two more months. We also lose a lot of time when the miners go back forth to Bishop or Laws to see their families. If we had family cabins up there, we would save a lot of time."

"I wonder if you could explain the mining process to me. I know little outside of what I have read."

"Well if you are like most people, you think gold is found in nuggets along streams. The truth is most gold is virtually invisible. You find most of it hidden in veins of quartzite or granite. The Gold Rush miners found gold dust or nuggets that eroded from rocks high up in the mountains and washed down in rivers and streams. That kind of gold exists, but it is rare. There are still old-timers panning along the streams, but their numbers are dwindling. In the old days they used hydraulic mining to wash the gold out of the alluvial deposit veins they found. They used high-powered hoses to wash the vein out of the rock and into large sluice boxes near a stream. They hoped to separate the gold from the "tailings" or excess materials. The larger gold mines use trammels to remove the larger alluvial material. We use some of those hydraulic processes ourselves at the mine, but we want to use a newer more efficient method."

"Tell me about the new method," Henry said.

"The new method uses a cyanide solution to mix with finely crushed rock to bring the gold to the surface. We use what are called stamping mills to crush the rock, which is usually quartzite. Much like a coal mine, the quartzite is mined using tunnels to get to the deeper veins of quartzite. They say the deeper you go with the mine the better the quality of gold. Once you get the quartzite out of the mine, it is taken to a stamping mill. The stamping mill has large pestles—heavy hammers made out of lead or steel—that are lifted by hydraulic machines then lowered to crush the rock. The pestles crush the rock into pebbles that fall through screens. The pebbles are then heated and mixed with cyanide or sometimes zinc, which teases out the gold. The gold melts and trickles into small lead containers that mold them into ingots."

"It sounds like an expensive process," Henry said. "You would think the more pestles you have the more gold you could process. Is that correct?"

"Theoretically, yes, but there is only so much quartzite to be found. You are also limited by your claims. We have only three claims we can mine at present. If you find gold, you can file a patent on the claim so no one else can work it. Last year we discovered a wide vein of gold in the center of one our claims. It contained dense, banded quartz carrying very fine gold. We did not have any way to separate the gold. If we had the necessary equipment and a large amount of cyanide and zinc, I believe we could bring 5,000 tons of quartzite to the surface next year. That would yield a fortune. In my opinion, this one vein we are working on will be one of the richest found in years. If we had more claims to work, I think Bishop Creek would be the most profitable mine in the United States."

"I know you can only estimate, but what would you guess the profit would be for every dollar spent?"

"My guess would be a return of $250 for every dollar spent."

Henry nearly stopped breathing. Could it be that he had found his fortune? Could he finally finance his magazine, his political career, and his future with Mary? Had he stumbled across an opportunity that would make his father's fortune seem trivial?

"Mr. Steiner, your words take my breath away."

"I know what we have here, Mr. Wilshire. None of the investors in New York have visited so I could explain it to them. For them this is a paper investment. I don't think they care if the mine produces. They only care if the stock sells. I assume the stock is not selling well, so they want to sell the mine. But the reason the mine is not doing well is because we have neither enough claims to mine nor the proper equipment."

"I promise you that if I decide to buy the mine you will have what you need. I cannot tell you how glad I am that I came to see the mine for myself. I can hardly wait to get started. Shall we go see the mine?"

"I have two horses waiting outside. I assume you can ride? You look fit to me."

"I am an accomplished horseman if I say so myself. I once saved a woman from falling off a cliff by overtaking a runaway horse."

"Well, these are workhorses, not racehorses. They can walk uphill for eight hours a day without tiring or even breaking a sweat. They are not beautiful, but they are indispensable."

The two horses were tethered to a post outside the hotel. Steiner was right, they were not beautiful thoroughbreds. But they did look incredibly strong with large rippling muscles and huge rumps. One was a dark brown mare and the other a gray stallion. There was also a pack mule loaded with supplies; Steiner did not want to waste a trip to town. The two men mounted the horses and started the long trek to the mine, which was at an elevation of 9000 feet. Bishop was at 4,200 feet, and Henry could already feel the altitude.

As the horses and riders climbed, the altitude began to affect Henry's breathing. There were only a few pines at this elevation but lots of aspen and birch trees with fresh spring leaves and brilliant white bark. Golden poppies dotted the trail, which ran next to a stream. Red-tailed hawks circled overhead, and the sound of chirping birds was intermittent. At one point Henry glimpsed a large coyote that still had its winter coat before the creature disappeared into the bushes.

BURIED TREASURE: *The rugged mountains at the top of the grade near the mine made transporting gold ore a difficult and costly proposition.*

About three hours into the ride, Steiner stopped at a beautiful spring near a meadow. He said they should rest the horses. He probably meant they should rest Henry, who was having difficulty catching his breath. Henry was a good horseman but was not used to such a steep climb. His thighs ached and his rump was asleep. He had brought riding gloves and boots, which helped, but this was different from riding in a park beside a beautiful woman.

The second leg of their journey would last another three hours. They could see the huge crevices of the gorgeous high mountains ahead. The stream along the road turned into a small river. Steiner said it was Bishop Creek, but Henry thought it was more of a river than a creek. You could hear the rushing of the white water as it cut through the dramatic landscape to the towns and the Owens River below.

Finally, the riders reached Cardinal Village, which was just a small number of tents, a tiny wooden cabin and a building that stored meat. Cardinal Village sat beside a small river and a creek. Steiner mentioned the large Sabrina Lake nearby and said North Lake, which was smaller, was about a half-mile north. Smoke was curling out of the cabin's stone chimney, and the smell of freshly baked bread filled the air, reminding Henry that he was famished. He and Steiner got off their horses, and a large, hearty-looking woman came out of the cabin to greet them. She said they were just about to serve supper. These were wonderful words to Henry.

Supper consisted of biscuits and gravy, a large slab of ham, potatoes, and a vegetable Henry did not recognize. A large pitcher of beer and a pot of coffee sat on each table. At one table, six men were being served family-style. The men, dirty and bearded, were obviously miners. Steiner introduced each of them to Henry.

"This here is Mr. Henry Wilshire, boys. He is thinking about buying the mine, so watch your language. Sing the mine's praises if you know what's good for you. I have been convincing him this the best mine in the country."

A small, skinny man wearing leather pants and a faded yellow miner's hat said, "Mr. Wilshire, if you want to make some money, this is the place. Just yesterday I took a nugget out of the wall as big as your fist. The gold in it was so pure you could see your face in it. I wanted it as a keepsake, but Tommy here said I needed to turn it in."

The man called Tommy said, "If you are buying lies, Mr. Wilshire, then Curley Joe here has a boatload for you. Mr. Wilshire, I have worked many a mine from here to Grass Valley, and I can tell you this mine is worth a fortune. We have only just begun to really tap the vein, and it is already paying off $5 a ton. Yesterday we mined 500 tons. Even Curley Joe can do the math. I would invest myself if I had the money."

"If I buy the mine, perhaps we can work out some way for you fellows to share in the profits. If I promise to stay out of the way, can you boys take me into the mine? I have come here to see for myself what this mine is all about. I am not a paper-and-pencil kind of investor. I will not interfere, but I want to see personally what I am getting into."

Steiner said, "I told Mr. Wilshire that we want an owner who takes a personal interest in the mine. He is aware of some of our needs. All joking aside, feel free to tell him your opinion of the mine's potential under the right ownership. Tell him about the problems as well. None of us wants to pull the wool over anyone's eyes."

A much older man seated at the end of the table said, "Mr. Wilshire, you seem like a pleasant enough man, so let me tell you what can go wrong in a gold mine."

"Please do," Henry replied.

"The most obvious is that you don't find any gold. There is an old saying among gold miners, 'Where it is, there it is, and where it is, there I ain't.' "

There was laughter all around.

"The second thing that can go wrong is you find gold but it ain't worth much. Not all gold is quality. Some if it is nothing but pyrite or 'fool's gold.' Pretty rocks are not worth bringing to the surface.

"The third is that it costs more to mine the gold than it is worth. You find a vein of gold in quartzite that is so hard it takes a fortune to tease the gold out. You won't make any money if you spend $25 an ounce extracting gold that you sell for $20 an ounce."

Henry said, "An old miner on the train warned me about that one. He said it was one of the main reasons mining companies go under."

"He told you right," the old-timer said. "Another thing that can go wrong is that a mine can go underwater for a spell due to melted snow. That is especially true up here. We don't have the necessary pumps. If we did, we could work more days per year."

Tommy said, "We all realize how helpful large pumps would be, but it will cost a lot of money to transport them to Laws and then up to the mine. Can you afford that, Mr. Wilshire?"

Henry was pleased at how candid the men were. "If I choose to buy the mine, I will sell shares to finance what we need. I can assure you men that I will also build a large cookhouse, a café, and cabins big enough for your families to join you."

That brought a cheer from the men in the room.

Steiner said, "Mr. Wilshire, you are already very popular around here. I think I speak for all the men when I say we need an owner like you."

"I promise to give you my best effort," Henry said. "I look forward to seeing the mine in the morning."

Exhausted from the ride, Henry collapsed into a comfortable bed in the lone cabin and woke at dawn. A coyote was howling in the distance and an owl was hooting outside the cabin window. He went downstairs and was surprised to see Steiner sitting at a table having coffee with a man Henry did not know. Steiner said good morning and introduced the newcomer as Rathbun, the mine foreman. Rathbun was rugged-looking, bearded and slightly dirty. Henry could smell the perspiration on his stained flannel shirt and the mud that caked his boots. Rathbun lit a small pipe, and fragrant tobacco smoke filled the air.

Rathbun, who oversaw the camp's ten miners, said the mine was producing about five tons of ore a day. He explained to Henry that they were using a combination of the old hydraulic process and the newer stamping and cyanide process. The hydraulic method was cheaper because water was readily available from Lake Sabrina. Cyanide was much more expensive

After another hearty breakfast, the three men set out on foot for the mine. They hiked along a stream and then across a small footbridge to a path that was covered with beautiful aspen leaves. They walked for about half an hour until they came to a wide, wooden bridge across a fast, cascading river. They stopped for a moment so Henry could take in the impressive view.

There was a slight chill in the air, and Henry was glad he had on a heavy coat. They walked another half-hour and approached a steep incline. Henry saw abandoned metal parts scattered here and there along the trail. He looked up a saw that the mountain emerged at a steep incline. The top of the mountain was covered with either snow or solid white granite. You could not see it clearly without a telescope. Finally they rounded a bend, and Henry saw what was to become his next obsession: the Bishop Creek Gold Mine. The entrance looked like a large cave about ten feet across and seven feet high at its highest point. The rock around it was brown and red. Steiner said this was the original mine dug ten years ago. The colored rock was actually iron ore that was rusting in the elements.

To the right and above the cave was a large wooden structure, where the stamping mill was located. Rathbun told Henry that stamp mills were originally developed in Cornwall, England, around 1850. The original stamps were primarily heavy timber on iron lifters with iron "heads" at the bottom. Cams on a rotating axle raised the heavy stamps, which then fell on the ore and crushed it into small lumps of sand-like material. The material was then filtered through a water wheel to flush out any gold. Henry had read about stamping mills, but it was beneficial to have the process explained by the miners. Henry was pleased to see that the stamp mill appeared to work perfectly, but he had no idea if they were finding any gold.

Steiner told Henry that the process would be more successful with more modern stamping machines that could hold as many as ten stamps at a time. They would also need steam instead of water wheels to lift the heavy stamps. The more stamping machines they had, the more ore they could process. Henry understood but wondered about hauling the equipment up that eighteen-mile road. Could mules pull that much weight up such a steep grade? Steiner assured him that with enough mules you could haul anything to the camp. Henry had his doubts but bowed to Steiner's expertise.

Henry was satisfied. He wanted this mine. He began turning over in his mind the idea of a syndicate that would sell stock in the mine. He knew he had many friends and business connections in Los Angeles, New York, and London who might be interested. He knew he could eventually raise enough money to buy bigger stamping machines and add steam power, pumps, and cabins. He could hardly wait to get back to New York to sell the mine to prospective investors.

As Henry and Steiner left the mine area, they approached an old miner sitting by a mule. "Mr. Wilshire, this is Three-Finger Jack," Steiner said. "He is the man who originally found the mine." Wilshire stepped forward and shook the old man's hand, pretending not to notice the missing fingers.

"Glad to meet you, Jack. How is it going up here? I cannot tell you how glad I am to be here."

Three-Finger Jack was not a sociable man. After too many years alone in the backcountry, his utterances were more croak than speech.

"Welcome to the best mine in the high Sierras," he rasped. "There is a fortune to be made if you have the gumption and the wherewithal to invest in this here mine."

Wilshire replied, "If you can show us where the gold is located, you need not worry about either my gumption or my wherewithal."

"Come on, Jack; let's show Mr. Wilshire where the gold is," Steiner said.

The three men hiked up a steep incline to the hole in the mountain. The ore was being taken from the side of the mountain by large elevators sunk into a large hole in the earth. Large wooden beams reinforced the entrance to the mine. They stepped inside, and the engineer lit a lantern.

They walked about twenty yards inside. Three-Fingered Jack said, "You see this here streak in the rock. That is quartzite and there is gold in that rock. City fellers like you expect to see gold nuggets sticking out of the wall, but that is not what gold looks like. Gold is like a good woman. You got to squeeze her gentle-like and talk to her nice before she will give you what you want. This mine will treat us real nice if we are careful with her."

Wilshire wasn't sure he liked the analogy, but he accepted that it took patience and know-how to extract gold from what looked like rock. The three men left the mine, and Henry shook the old man's hand and thanked him for his advice.

As they came down the hill, they heard a loud thump, then another, and another coming from the wooden structure. They could see smoke coming from a metal barrel. They looked into the building, and Henry saw a large stamping hammer rising and falling onto the rock on a screen. The stamp made a loud noise as it struck the rock and splintered it into hundreds of pebbles. Henry had to stand back to avoid the spraying rock fragments. Steiner gave him a pair of goggles to wear. The pebbles were falling into a large boiling cauldron. A man was shoveling different sand-like substances into the vat. It reminded Henry of watching the men make steel in Ohio. He could not tell if there was any gold coming out of the mixture at the bottom, but he remembered that Steiner had told him gold was invisible. Besides, a few ounces of gold would not look like much.

He and Steiner walked back to the lodge. He liked Steiner and knew he was lucky to have found a chief engineer who was both skilled and respectable. He also loved the setting and could not wait to tell Mary about the area. It was the most beautiful place he had ever seen, and the entire experience was too good to be true. Perhaps he could build a house for Mary up here. He thought she would love it.

Henry returned to New York, and by June 1906 the Bishop Creek Gold Mine had a new set of officers and directors—nearly all of them socialists. James Gilfillan was president; W.B McReynolds (Wilshire's father in-law), vice president; A.A. Hassan (a mineralogist), consulting engineer; G.W. Wilkins, managing engineer; and Henry, secretary/treasurer. Wilshire's company began offering stock at $2.50 a share. Its executive offices would be in New York City, and there would be a local office in Bishop. He began publishing articles in *Wilshire's Magazine* that called Bishop Creek the "World's Greatest Mine" and the Tip Top claim a "mountain of solid ore." Stock sold rapidly in the United States and England. By 1907 the company had sold $2.6 million worth of shares.

Henry built a village of small cabins for the men and a home for Mary and himself near the mine. He purchased 99 claims and patented 12 of them. He also bought a large water pump and had it shipped from Los Angeles up to the mine. He had plans to increase the number of stamps to ten but would have to wait until in the company could afford it.

In 1907 he decided to protect his investment by forming the Bishop Creek Milling Company. This company would own stock in the Bishop Creek Gold Mine but would have a separate board. Henry made himself president. The second company started with $200,000 in capital. Its profits came strictly from gold, not stock ventures. If the stock ventures went under, Henry would still have the gold mine.

A ten-stamp mill was built in 1908. Snow slides and snow melt continued to hamper mining. They decided to build a tramway 50 feet higher than the mine so a continuous flow of ore could travel downhill. In 1910 a miner called Old Mib was hired to build a road up to Lake Sabrina above the mine. He proceeded to blast away the obstacles, but the road was incredibly steep. A wagon could go up the road, but if it tried to come down the incline, the wagon would crush the horse. Old Mib solved the problem by driving a huge steel stake in the ground and winching the wagons and horses down the road. He called it "Cable Hill."

After Old Mib completed his road, he accidentally found gold across the stream from the Bishop Creek mine. He staked a claim and told Henry he could have the claim in exchange for a truckload of whiskey. Wilshire obliged, and poor Old Mib died trying to drink it all in three days.

INCORPORATED UNDER THE LAWS OF ARIZONA
NUMBER 4943
WILSHIRE
Bishop Creek Company
=150= SHARES
SHARES $ 5.00 EACH
CAPITAL STOCK $ 25,000,000.
SHARES FULL PAID AND NON-ASSESSABLE
This Certifies that GEORGE L. VANELLIS is the owner of --ONE HUNDRED FIFTY-- Shares of the Capital Stock of the Wilshire Bishop Creek Company, transferable only on the Books of the Company in person or by Attorney upon surrender of this Certificate. In Witness Whereof, the duly authorized officers of the Company have hereunto subscribed their names and caused the corporate Seal to be hereto affixed this 21st day of February 1910.
TREASURER
VICE PRESIDENT

Courtesy of Scriptophilly Documents
CEASE AND DESIST: *In 1910, the Wilshire Bishop Creek Company was ordered to stop selling stock until an investigation could examine the complaints of some London investors that the mine did not exist.*

In 1909 Wilshire issued plans to build a hydraulic water plant at the mill. The next year a group of disgruntled London investors accused Henry of conning them and charged that the mine did not exist. In June 1910, the U.S. Post Office was alerted, and it ordered the Wilshire Bishop Creek Company to close down the mine if there was one and stop selling shares. The officials accused Wilshire of fraud for allegedly using funds raised from the mine for purposes other than mining. The charge likely referred to Wilshire's advertising mining stock in *Wilshire's*, his socialist magazine. The Postal Service sent an inspector out to investigate. The inspector never went anywhere near the mine and did not question bankers or anyone else in Bishop about it. There was some question as to whether he even went to Bishop. Yet the inspector reported that the mine did not exist. After the citizens of Bishop protested, the government dropped the case in 1911. The postmaster general sent Henry a letter expressing his apologies and his confidence in the mine.

While the U.S. government and London newspapers were calling him a swindler and a cheat, Henry was traveling between London and his two gold mines in British Guiana. Wilshire had purchased the Aremu and Tassawini gold mines in 1910, and they actually yielded more gold than Bishop Creek did. In the end, they were sold to support the Bishop Creek mine and pay debts.

By the time the investigation was completed, the mine was underwater, and it took months of pumping before it was operational again. There was so much snow in the winter that flooding of the mine and surrounding area was common once the weather started to warm up. Additional pumps could keep the water out of the mine, but that required money.

In 1915 Wilshire built a large, lovely stone home just above Cardinal Village. It was on a rise with views of the valley below and the mountains to the west. It was a lovely spot. In fall the white aspen leaves turned yellow, and the entire landscape appeared to be made of gold. Mary loved the area and made many friends. She spent more time there than Henry did.

That year the mine produced 5,000 tons of ore, which yielded about $55,000—not enough for the mining operation to be profitable. The miners built several shafts, one as deep as 300 feet. To produce that much ore, the 1,000 feet of workings in the mine had extracted 13,138 tons of quartzite and granite. Of course, the cost exceeded the profits. Unable to find new investors, Wilshire was forced to close the mine in 1916. He tried to resurrect it in 1920 but was unsuccessful. By then an entirely different process involving gyratory crushers, rod mills, and classifiers had modernized the gold mining process and had increased the yield of gold from quartzite. Henry had neither the money nor the knowledge to adopt the new methods. He finally leased the property to the Consolidated Mining Company, which modernized the mine and returned it to operation on a limited basis.

Consolidated Mining had the capital to innovate, and it made a sizable profit before the mountain's supply of gold ore seemed to dry up. The mine stood idle between 1924 and 1928. Consolidated Mining sold the mine, and it was later bought and sold several times over. The fabled mine finally ceased operations in August 1938. In its total time in operation, the mine produced approximately $1.6 million in gold—a sizable amount in 1930 dollars, but the debts may have exceeded its profits.

Like many of his ventures, he over-promised and under-produced. Wilshire sold more shares in the mine than it was worth, and he diverted funds to his magazine instead of paying dividends to stockholders or reinvesting in the mine. His biggest fault was failing to heed the warnings that the cost of extracting the gold would exceed its value. Many would call Henry a cheat, but there is little doubt that Henry thought every shareholder would eventually profit, including himself. Optimism was Henry's trademark. He may have been naïve, but many gold seekers have made the same mistakes.

New Road to Good Health

Learn What Wilshire's

I-ON-A-CO

May Do For You

No Bathing—No Sweating—No Electrifying
No Dieting—No Psychologizing—No Exercising
No Drugging—No Faith-Curing
No Manipulating

Wilshire's IONACO is an electro-magnetic appliance which you attach to an electric light socket and place around your body over your clothing, as shown in the illustration. It magnetizes the iron in your body and thus increases oxygen brought to the tissue cells. This oxidation purifies the blood stream and tends to restore the Ionaco user to perfect health.

Call at our offices for a FREE DELIGHTFUL TREATMENT, or telephone us for a free demonstration at your home.

I-on-a-co has given her hair, formerly perfectly straight, a natural and permanent wave.

FREE LECTURES
by Gaylord Wilshire, Inventor of I-ON-A-CO—
In San Francisco—EVERY TUESDAY at 3 p. m. and 8:15 p. m.
and FRIDAY EVENINGS at 8:15
In Oakland—EVERY THURSDAY at 3 p. m. and at 8:15 p. m.
Also on the air OVER KTAB EVERY THURSDAY, 5:45 to 6:15
If you live out of town, send for free booklet

SAN FRANCISCO:
3d Floor, Elevated Shops
150 Powell St.
Telephone Kearny 3802

Wilshires I·ON·A·CO

OAKLAND:
3d Floor, Ray Building
1924 Broadway
Telephone Lakeside 385

CHAPTER 8
Pasadena and the I- On- A- Co Belt

The Bishop Creek Gold Mine was not furnishing the capital for his magazine like Henry had hoped. It was like the old saying about boats; they are a hole in the water to put money into. The magazine was like that. It took more and more money to keep the magazine going. He increased the amount of advertising space. Nothing seemed to help. Finally he decided to insert advertisements for his Bishop Creek Gold Mine. He hoped the advertisements would increase the sales of stock in the mine which he turn could use to keep the magazine going. He knew if the stockholders found out what he was doing he would be in trouble. The magazine was worth the risk. Eugene Debs, the socialist leader at the time, advised him against placing ads for his gold mine in a socialist magazine. If the mine did not produce, his socialist comrades would hold him responsible. It was not good to mix ownership in a gold mine with socialism.

Henry ignored Debs' advice and in 1910 the Post Office again accused him of using Wilshire Magazine to promote fraudulent claims for a gold mine that did not exist. It turned out that Debs was right, and many of the claims against Wilshire to the federal government came from socialist investors in the mine. They called him a fake and a swindler. It looked like Wilshire could be fined heavily or worse, he could be sent to jail for fraud. Henry and Mary escaped to Hampstead Heath, England. Henry traveled to British Guiana to check on the progress of his two gold mines there and discovered that that one of them mines was worthless and the other was producing better than Bishop Creek. He managed to sell them both, and he and Mary and Logan had enough to live on for another few years. Henry and Mary lived in Hampstead for three years, and Mary began studying the new field of psychoanalysis in Zurich. Finally, in 1911 Henry received a letter from Postmaster J.W. Clark of Bishop saying the case against him had been dropped. Much of the case for him was from citizens of Bishop stating his efforts to work the mine were legitimate.

Wilshire's Magazine had sold fewer and fewer copies of since London, Sinclair and Shaw stopped submitting articles. The bigger issue was that socialism was no longer interesting to much of the public. Henry was forced to stop the publication, and the last issue was published in April 1914.

By 1914 Henry had become somewhat disillusioned with socialism and became more interested in syndicalism. Syndicalism was an alternative to socialism in the United States and Britain. Syndicalists believed in replacing capitalism with a federation of industrial trade unions. It also believed the people had a better chance with the trade unions managing the economy than with a socialist government. Before his death in 1916, Jack London became a syndicalist as well. His friend Upton Sinclair was still active in socialist circles and kept him in touch with key leaders in New York, Chicago and Los Angeles.

Mary had been studying in Zurich before the war and had difficulty getting back to England. She was forced to flee Europe through France and Spain and then take a ship to London. She told stories about how the ship had to avoid being torpedoed. After the war she continued her studies with a physician named Sigmund Freud and one his associates, Karl Jung. When the war began in 1914, Henry moved Mary and their young eight-year-old son, Logan, to Bishop. While Mary and Logan enjoyed their time in Bishop and at the Cardinal Village near the mine, Henry tried to regain the fortune he had lost. He left Mary and Logan at Cardinal Village and returned to Los Angeles.

When Henry returned to Los Angeles he found his name printed across the titles of dozens of churches, insurance companies, hotels and restaurants. He wrote Shaw a letter that he found it somewhat humorous that his name was associated with so many churches when he was an atheist. He also wrote to Shaw that it was too bad there was not more money attached to people using his name. He might be a rich man. He tried real estate speculation, a health food store, and a health spa. He even tried selling vacuum cleaners for a time. Nothing did well. Henry still believed Southern California was the land of opportunity.

He purchased a small piece of property in Pasadena. The property was a five-acre orange grove with a small house. It had a lovely view of the San Gabriel Mountains. He moved Mary and Logan to Pasadena.

Pasadena in 1916 still had many dirt roads. Colorado Boulevard was paved and had a streetcar track down the middle. The streetcar line connected Pasadena with downtown Los Angeles. The light rail system was designed by Henry Huntington, who had built a large home in the town of Arcadia near Pasadena.

Lake Street, a wide north-south road in the eastern part of the city, was still dirt. It had stone curbs and a wooden board-walk. Streetlights were scattered throughout the new city, which was becoming an attraction for the rich and the famous. Large homes were built along Orange Grove Avenue for the rich. There was a technical college near the downtown area, and a stadium that had football games during the fall and track meets in the spring. A wonderful parade was held on New Year's Day, featuring floats full of flowers and lovely girls. It was a city that was blossoming. Henry believed that he would hold on to the Pasadena house for a few years and then sell it for a large profit.

Mary McReynolds was pleased when she found out that Henry had purchased a house in Pasadena. She was not one that needed a large mansion. She had studied with Jung in Switzer-land and had also taken classes with Freud. She had become a well-known authority on psychoanalysis, giving lectures all over the United States. She started a practice in Brentwood, not too far from their Pasadena home. She was secretly glad that Henry was disillusioned with socialism. Perhaps now they could settle down to a normal life. Mary did so well in her practice that she was able to save enough money to buy a small house in Palm Springs, a tiny desert community about fifty miles east of Pasadena. She saw it as a personal retreat for herself. She became the main source of income for the family. This was difficult for Henry.

Los Angeles after the First World War was a place full of faith healers, health fanatics and pseudoscientific miracle workers. It was a time of Amy Semple McPherson, who healed blindness, paralysis and other major ailments with acts of prayer. It was a time of magic potions that consisted of 20 percent alcohol and secret ingredients made by the pharaohs. It was the time of gadgets, and con men and made-to-order get-rich-quick gimmicks. Magazines were full of advertisements for health potions and inventions that promised all sorts of cures.

When Henry moved to Pasadena his migraine headaches increased both in intensity and frequency. Part of the pain was probably due the fact that he lost all his money on the Bishop Creek Gold Mine and *Wilshire's Magazine*. Henry found the pain in his head was so bad that he was forced to his bed. Medicines and doctors were no help. There seemed to be no relief. Mary McReynolds was also ill at times, with one respiratory infection after another. Henry was now nearly sixty years old and found that eighteen holes of golf tired him and he could not take long hikes anymore. Henry had always been an active man, both physically and spiritually. He needed something to keep his mind busy.

Henry and Mary had many friends, many of them from their old socialist circles. There was a wealthy Pasadena socialite by the name of Kate Crane Gertz. Mrs. Gertz was known as the wealthy grande dame of Pasadena and was a whirlwind of energy. Her parties included leading artists and movie actors. Many of her guests had socialist leanings. Many did not, which made for interesting conversation. She once bailed Upton

Sinclair out of jail. Henry and Mary were often invited to her garden parties. Guests included Charlie Chaplin, H.G. Wells, King Gillette, Igor Paderewski, Pablo Casals, Lord Russell, Douglas Fairbanks, and George Westinghouse Jr., who was the son of George Westinghouse, the great inventor. Other famous guests for tea were Frank Lloyd Wright, Bobby Scripps, and Cornelius Vanderbilt Jr. The Wilshire attended the teas but had luncheons of the their own that included H.G. Wells, Charmain London, Mother Jones, Julian Hawthorne, Rebecca West, Lincoln Stephens and Peggy Wood.

George Westinghouse and Henry found they had something in common in terms of wanting to find an invention that would make a lot of money. They frequently had lunch together in a small cafe in downtown Pasadena. There was an engineer named Van Kuran who taught at California Technological College and lunched with them at times.

At one of those luncheons they were discussing new health inventions, and Van Kuran mentioned that there is a great deal of iron in the bloodstream and that there had been efforts to use electricity to activate the iron. Some scientists believed manipulating the iron in the bloodstream could cure many kinds of illnesses. Van Kuran also told them radium was being tried for a whole series of ailments, and he suggested that Henry try a radium cap to see if that would help his migraines.

Henry's friend Upton Sinclair had told him about a machine called "The Autoclast" that sounded similar to what Van Kuran had described. The luncheon meetings and conversations between Westinghouse and Van Kuran were just what the fertile and creative mind of Henry Gaylord Wilshire needed. He began to read and talk to scientists, physicians and engineers about ways to influence the iron in the blood. He looked at many of the gadgets and inventions that were being advertised in magazines to cure diabetes, cancer, baldness and constipation. He knew that if he could invent a machine that could influence the iron in the blood, he might be able to help cure ailments at least as well as or better than those advertised. He thought he needed to invent a device that used electrical energy to attract the ions in the bloodstream.

Henry thought the device needed to be simple and easy to use. It also had to be lightweight and attractive. He worked with Van Kuran and came up with a device that met his needs. He had heard of a company called The Ex- cell –o-bread Company and he liked to sound of the name. He decided to call his device the I-on-a-co Magnetic Belt.

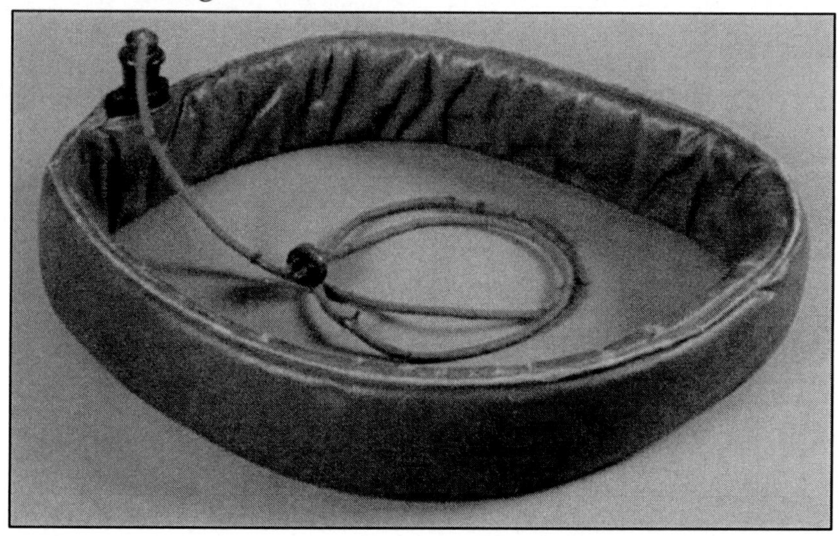

The belt went through a number of trials and experiments. He designed two brown leatherette-covered coils of insulated wire. The smaller coil would have two free ends attached to a miniature light socket with a 7-volt light bulb. The large coil would be thickly padded and have an electric cord with a two-prong plug. The person using the belt would only need to place the "horse collar-like "device over their shoulder or across their lap and plug it in.

Henry believed that if the user plugged in the device for ten minutes once or twice a day it would magnetize the blood and cure many minor and perhaps major ailments. He was the first to test the gadget. He found it made his headaches less severe and less frequent. He tried the belt on Mary, and she found that she had fewer colds. He gave one to several friends for various ailments, and they said the results were miraculous.

One of his friends said it lessened his cancer. Another said it helped him grow hair. Numerous friends said it helped with constipation. Very few were negative about the apparatus. It certainly did no harm.

Henry was not a physician or an engineer. He wasn't a mining engineer or a publisher either but the lack of credentials never bothered him. After several failed experiments and a great deal of consultation with others, Henry began manufacturing the I-On-A-Co. His friend George Westinghouse Jr. had the belts made at his Los Angeles plant.

Never short on ego and self-promotion, Henry used his somewhat recognizable name and placed advertisements for the belt in local newspapers.

This ad ran in the *Los Angeles Times*: "Gaylord Wilshire was educated at Harvard and came of a family of doers and go-getters. Mr. Wilshire's virtues, as summarized are: social crusader, magazine publisher, gold miner, explorer, pioneer city builder, tropical explorer, lecturer, writer, friend and companion of great authors, artists, luminaries of the drama and stage in Europe and America, and now inventor of a magnetic appliance that is banishing pain and suffering from thousands of his fellow men, not to mention causing a veritable revolution the whole field of therapy."

Henry gave the following directions on how to use the belt: "If you will stand the Belt up against the back of a chair and then sit on the chair with the ring over your chest, the bulb will become illuminated, showing the passage of magnetism clearing through your body. Be careful not to put the test ring too close to the Belt, otherwise you will burn out the bulb. I am also enclosing a buzzer, which may be attached to the ring and which will operate about the same as the light." After a few months, testimonials by customers who had tried the belt started to arrive.

J. Smith of Los Angeles said, "I have suffered from arthritis for eleven years. I used the Ion-a-co. The lime has dissolved in the joint of my hip and I have regained my health completely. In addition my white hair had become black again."

Jim Rowan of Los Angeles exclaimed, "I was diagnosed as dying of heart disease. I was given up as incurable by a prominent physician. I tried the I-on-a-co and now I am well. I have no sign of heart disease."

Mrs. Jane Griswold of Los Angeles stated, "I have suffered from diabetes Mellitus for two and a half years. I used the I-on-a-co and now eat whatever I want including candy and deserts. I am cured."

E.K. Cassan, a fruit packer, wrote Wilshire," I was paralyzed from the waist down, my legs being always cold. I used the I-on-a-co and my circulation had been restored and I can walk again."

Frank Similar of Los Angeles said simply, "I have been cured of my cancer by the I-on-a-co."

There were testimonials from nearly a hundred of Henry's friends and acquaintances as well as the general public. Henry was convinced that the Belt worked and that he had found a major breakthrough that would help millions. There were written and verbal testimonials about how the Belt had cured Bright's disease, dropsy, pernicious anemia, goiter, mental derangement, varicose veins, gallstones, prostrate trouble, and canine chorea. A dog was cured of St. Vitus dance by sleeping close to the belt while it was on. Why wouldn't he believe the belt worked when there were so many testimonials?

Henry advertised profusely in newspapers and magazines throughout the country. He even went on the new radio to plug his product. The orders poured in, and he could hardly make the belts fast enough to satisfy the demand.

Wilshire had to hire sales reps in various cities. The I-on-a-co Company had offices in Oakland, Los Angeles, San Francisco, San Diego, Berkeley, Long Beach, Chicago, Portland, Seattle, Tacoma, Denver, Kansas City, Palo Alto, Alhambra and Cincinnati. He sold the belt to his sales agents for half price, and they turned around and sold it for full price. The belt sold for $58.50 cash or $65 on time. The belt cost Wilshire less than $5 to make.

The belt made more money than Bishop Creek Gold Mine and *Wilshire's Magazine* put together. One of the things that Henry Gaylord Wilshire was best at was selling things. He gave workshops to his sales force in various cities as to how to sell and market the belt. He even encouraged his son, Logan, on one of his many trips to Italy, to see if he could arrange an audience with Benito Mussolini. Mussolini had frequent headaches, and Henry was certain the belt could help him. (Logan was never able to set up a meeting with Mussolini.)

Henry encouraged businesses to give the belt away as a sales promotion. One gas station owner in Portland offered a free belt to anyone who filled up and had an oil change. Henry redesigned the belt, reducing its weight from 7 pounds to 2 pounds.

In 1926, Wilshire sold 400 belts a day. He sold 30,000 in 1926 alone. By April 1927 he had sold 50,000 Belts and had nearly a million dollars in profit. The Gold Mine and *Wilshire's Magazine* were defunct, so Wilshire bought a small beach house in Santa Monica.

There were a number of studies on the value of the belt. One study by Dr. Arthur J. Ramp summarizes a description of the belt in *The Hygeia Journal* for Feb. 1927. The study stated, " The I-on-a Belt is simply a coil of insulated wire (about 6 lb. of 22 gage worth about $3.50) with a plug that permits the coil to be attached to an electric light socket. When it is plugged into an electric socket there is an alternating current that generates a weak fluctuating magnetic field. When that occurs a small flashlight bulb lights up. The entire cost could not have exceeded $5.00 in materials."

On the other side a noted physician said, "Although the electromagnetic current of the Belt was is not sufficient to cure major diseases, if it is applied to accupoints it could remediate minor ailments like fatigue, hemorrhoids, goiter, earaches, stiff necks and sore throats."

A group of physical therapists and sports doctors were experimenting with the use of electrical stimulus to help with curing sports injuries. Those machines were not much different from the I-on-a-co belt.

A gullible public was willing to believe in miracles and healers. The facts about the belt did not lessen its sales. Besides, the experts were divided on its worth. It seemed the wilder the claims for the belt the more people wanted it.

Earl John Russell, the brother of Bertrand Russell, knew Wilshire and said "I would rather be killed by a doctor than cured by a quack." Thousands disagreed with him. One of Wilshire's reporter friends wrote him, "Thanks for giving me the best laugh I have had for a long time. Every boob will want one of your Belts." Wilshire sent a belt to Clarence Darrow. Darrow returned it, saying, "I think I have lived too long already."

Wilshire tried to get a patent on the belt. The patent office twice refused his application. They gave no reason in their rejection slips.

Because there was no patent, a number of knockoffs began to appear. One, called the Theronoid, was identical to the I-on-a-co. It was manufactured and sold by Philip Isley, the onetime manager of Wilshire's Cleveland office.

In the end the success of the belt was its undoing. Wilshire wrote to his friend George Bernard Shaw at one point "I have an absolute monopoly on the field in magnetism for health purposes." He was wrong. By 1925 there were fifty companies selling knockoffs of the I-on-a-co.

Wilshire also experimented with radium mixed with silk thread. He believed the radium-infused silk could create a cure for certain ailments, including menstrual cramps. He experimented with a radium cap that could be worn to cure headaches and perhaps baldness. He found a textile manufacturer who was interested in the idea, but Wilshire died before developing the products.

By 1926 there began to be serious criticism of the belt by members of the medical profession. The Public Health League of Washington, working in cooperation with the Better Business Bureau of Seattle, formed a committee of experts, including a technician from an X-ray company; the secretary of the State Pharmacy Association; the Secretary of the Public Health League; two physicians, both of whom were specialists in physical therapy; the dean of the college of engineering of the state university; the commissioner of health of Seattle; and the construction engineer of the City Light Department of Seattle. The committee reported that "The I-on-a-co belt as a cure for any physical ailment was not worth five cents." The California Medical Association also began to condemn the belt as a fraud.

Wilshire became defensive and published an advertisement in the *Los Angeles Times* in February of 1926 which stated, "Since 1925 I have been advertising my invention, the I-on-a-co Belt, in practically all the leading newspapers in California. I have been broadcasting weekly lectures regarding the I-on-a-co over three radio stations. I have lectured in person in many California cities. In these advertisements I have made such statements as: 'If you are suffering from pain -- no matter what the cause -- one treatment may bring complete relief, as it has in hundreds of cases. Eczema relieved overnight. High blood pressure - we reduce in one treatment. Neuritis relieved in ten minutes.' In making such statements, I am either a liar a quack, or I am not. Either the I-on-a-co Belt is a fake, or it is not. If it is a fake it is the duty of the medical profession of California to denounce me and my invention as such."

Wilshire made a bad mistake when he made elaborate claims that the belt that had been endorsed by the Rockefeller Institute for Medical Research. He also published a long list of testimonials attributed to well-known physicians. The American Medical Association investigated those purported testimonials and found that they were false.

The Rockefeller Institute launched an investigation into the belt. Before the report was completed, Wilshire died of heart disease in his apartment in New York City at the age of 66. Thus ended one of Wilshire's most successful schemes and business ventures. Whether it was a fraud or not is best left to others to determine. There is little doubt that Wilshire thought the belt worked.

Epilogue

Henry stared out at the ocean. He loved sitting on the beach at dawn watching the surf and thinking. He let his mind wander over his entire life. Some days he focused on the bad things that had happened to him and people who had slighted or demeaned him in some way. Other mornings he thought about people he loved and the joys of having good friends, a good wife and a fine son. Some days it was a mix of the two.

Henry was not afraid to die, and he knew that his life was coming to a close. He was in good health as far as he knew but he was sixty-six and his father had died at age sixty-five. Mary was his pride and joy and he loved her as much as he had ever loved anyone. She was a good person, and that summed up most of what he loved about her. She had many friends and acquaintances, and she sincerely cared about other people. She especially cared about him, and he knew it.

There many things in his life that he was proud of doing. He recalled how he had run for Congress three times, for attorney general of New York, and Parliament in Great Britain and Canada. He did not expect to win in any of those political contests, but the fact that it irritated the establishment brought him secret pleasure.

He was also proud of *Wilshire's Magazine*. In its heyday it was a major socialist journal and featured articles by some of the world's great socialist writers.

He was proud that he knew Jack London, Upton Sinclair and George Bernard Shaw. He was not so proud of the fact that he owed them money and had no way to pay them.

He was proud of Wilshire Boulevard and what it had become. He could not have imagined how important that thirty-five-acre plot had become. As an atheist, he thought it odd that so many churches on the boulevard used his name. The last time he looked there were at least twenty with the name Wilshire on their billboard.

He was disappointed that some people thought he was a cheat and a charlatan. When critics wrote that his I-on-a-co belt was a worthless fraud, it hurt him. He seriously believed that the belt worked and that it helped people. Perhaps some of it was all in their minds, but what of it? The fact was that it helped thousands of people.

He hated to hear criticism of his management of the Bishop Creek Gold Mine. People said he sold phony stock. They said he knew the mine would never produce enough gold for the dollar amount of stock that he sold. The fact was, until the day he had to close the mine he still expected the mine to produce. He fully intended to pay every investor what he owed them. Someday someone would be able to make the mine pay a dividend. He had neither the time nor the resources to make that happen.

Overall he was satisfied that he had gotten a lot out of his life. He had been married twice, had a wonderful son and numerous friends. Those were the basics that really mattered. He was well known by many people throughout the world. He had published books and magazines that had played a small part in promoting socialist causes. He knew he would never be known as a great man, but he hoped he would be remembered as an interesting man.

One of Henry's great disappointments was that he was not able to help the poor and the working man and woman as much as he would have liked. He believed that the majority of Americans lived below the poverty line in poor housing and received poor wages while the large trusts and greedy individuals owned most of the wealth of America. He had always been more interested in helping the working poor than in acquiring personal wealth.

During the last few years he was concerned for his own family's economic welfare. He knew Mary's psychoanalysis practice was doing well and that she could support herself and Logan if something should happen to him.

He was disappointed with socialism in the United States. He now believed it would never blossom in America. The average American would not accept socialism unless they were in much more desperate financial circumstances. Americans are just simply not poor enough to want socialism. They were pragmatic and wanted government programs that protected them from extreme poverty or illness, but they would never agree to level the playing field as far as wealth was concerned.

Wilshire hoped that he would live long enough to see some of his ideas such as social security and health care for all, workman's compensation and unemployment insurance come into being. These were ideas he wrote about in *Wilshire's Magazine*. They were not his ideas alone, but he certainly gave them lots of words in print at a time when they were mostly new ideas.

Henry was pleased that many people called him a prophet. He knew in a sense he was a prophet. He was certainly a prophet in predicting that Los Angeles would become a great city and that the automobile would be a part of that growth.

The sun was beginning to go down along the horizon. The blue skies had become pink with shades of red. Henry stood up from the beach chair on which he had been sitting and stared out at the sea.

He always loved the sound of the waves as they broke along the shore. He saw the breakers curl and then drop their load of water and foam into the swirling tidal flow moving out from the shore to meet the breakers. The sound of the breakers was wonderful.

All that energy. He knew it was caused by the pull of the moon on the water and that it would last forever. He couldn't help wonder why all that energy could not be harnessed somehow. There had to be a way to capture that energy and turn it into electricity. He wondered if anyone had tried that yet. He thought he would call George Westinghouse Jr. and ask if there was any way to capture the energy of the tides and turn it into energy that could be sold. There was a lot of money to be made if he could be the first to find a way to do it. He knew nothing about physics, but so what? This could be the best idea of this life. He couldn't wait to get started.

References

Much of the reference material for this book came from thirty-five boxes of letters at the UCLA Library, Department of Special Collection, Charles E. Young Library. There were also five boxes of letters from the Huntington Library Department of Special Collection that were primarily letters between Henry Wilshire and Jack London. Historical collections at the Santa Monica Library, Pasadena Library, Long Beach Library and Los Angeles Public Library were also helpful.

Baldwin, Leland, *The Stream of American History* (American Book Co., New York, 1952)

Baster, Fred, *Great American Billboards* (Ten Speed Press, 2007)

Bausum, Ann, *Muckrakers* (National Geographic Society, Washington, D.C., 2007)

Dash, Norman, *Yesterday's Los Angeles* (Turner Publishing, Nashville, TN, 2008)

Dicher, Mau, *The Chinese in San Francisco* (Dover Publishing, New York, 1979)

Dumpke, Glen, *The Boom of the Eighties* (Huntington Library, Arcadia, CA, 1944)

Evans, Judith, *The Politics and Plays of George Bernard Shaw* (McFalan and Co., London, 2003)

Gilman, Jane, "Wilshire Boulevard Milestones," www.wilshirecenter.com/history

Grace, Roger M., "Reminiscing," Metropolitan News-Enterprise, May 19, 2011

Hancock, Ralph, *Fabulous Blvd.* (Funk and Wagnall's, 1949)

Hill, Eldon, *George Bernard Shaw* (Twayne Publications, Boston, 1978)

Hill, Joseph P., *Hill's Manual of Social and Business Forms*, New York, 1873

Holroyd, Michael, *The Genius of Shaw* (Holt Rinehart and Winston, New York, 1979)

Kemble, John Haskell, *San Francisco Bay, A Pictorial Maritime History* (Bonaventure Press, 1957)

Leadabrand, Russ; Shelly Lowenkopf, Bryce Patterson, *Yesterday's California* (Seemann Publishing, Miami, 1975)

Mayo, Morrow, *Los Angeles* (Alfred Knopf, New York, 1932)

Muscatine, Doris, *Old San Francisco, The Biography of a City* (G.P. Putnam's Sons, New York, 1975)

Nadeau, Remi, *Los Angeles: From Mission to Modern City* (Longmans Green and Co., New York, 1960)

Nadeau, Rami, *City Makers* (Trans-Anglo Books, 1965)

Nakashima, Signe E., *Cardinal Mine: A Ghost of the Past*, (Community Printing and Publishing, Bishop, CA, 1995)

Nelson, Howard J., (ed.), *The Los Angeles Metropolis*, 1978

O'Flaherty, Joseph S., *Those Powerful Years* (Historical Society of Southern California, 1992)

Quint, Howard, *The Forging of American Socialism* (American Heritage series, 1953)

Raskin, Jonah (ed.), *The Radical Jack London* (University of California Press, 2008)

Roderick, Kevin, *Wilshire Blvd.* (Angel City Press, San Diego, 2005)

Sinclair, John, *San Francisco, A Cultural and Literary History* (Interlink Books, New York, 2004)

Smith, Page, *The Rise of Industrial America, vol. 6* (Penguin Books, New York, 1984)

Starr, Kevin, *California* (Modern Library Chronicles Book, 2005)

Starr, Kevin, *Inventing the Dream* (Oxford Press, 1985)

Sinclair, Mick, *San Francisco* (Interlink Books, New York, 2004)

Wachs, Martin, *Autos, Transit, and the Sprawl of Los Angeles*, 1983

Wilshire, Logan, "Unpublished Biography of his Father," UCLA Department of Special Collection, Charles E. Young Library, Los Angeles, 1957

The World Wide Web was enormously helpful in providing factual information for this book. Hundreds of websites were used. Wikipedia was always the most useful.

Photo Credits –

Photos were taken from the collections of the following institutions or libraries with permission. Photos without a courtesy credit were in the public domain as far as could be determined. The author wishes to thank the staff of the various libraries and research institutions for their generous help and support.

The Library of Congress Photo Collection

The Center for the History of Political Economy at Duke University

The Charles E. Young Department of Special Collections at UCLA

The Huntington Library Digital Collection

The Bancroft Library Collection

The Long Beach Library Historical Collection

The Santa Monica Historical Museum

The Seaver Center for Western History Research/ Natural History Museum of Los Angeles County

Security Pacific National Bank Collection/Los Angeles Public Library

Society of California Pioneers

The California Historical Society

Don's Cards – Cincinnati, Ohio

Scripophily Historical Documents

Local History Room Fullerton Public Library

Stanford Library Photo Collection

The Warren J. Samuels Portrait Collection at Duke University

Stanford University, Libraries, Dept. of Special Collections

John P. Haynes Foundation

Wikipedia was a source for many photographs in the public
domain.